Adventures
in Contemporary Yucatán

An American's Reflections

Adventures in Contemporary Yucatán
An American's Reflections

Alan Van Bodegraven

Published by The Write Place
Pella, Iowa

Published in the United States of America by The Write Place

The Write Place
599 228th Place
Pella, Iowa 50219
www.thewriteplace.biz

Photos by Alan Van Bodegraven
Cover design by Victoria Watson
Page design by Alexis Thomas

ISBN: 978-0-9800084-3-2

Preface

For the first two thirds of my life I had never heard of the Yucatán and was only vaguely aware of there being pyramids and temples of an ancient civilization somewhere in some jungles in Mexico. That scant knowledge was probably the result of my poring over the National Geographic magazines that my grandparents passed on to me. My special interest was always the maps included, but occasionally I glanced at some of the articles also. Through a series of unplanned twists and turns in my personal and professional lives, I have spent the better part of this last third of my life (so far!) traveling throughout the Yucatán peninsula of Mexico and eventually living amongst the city *meztisos* and rural indigenous Maya. It has been a life-changing experience, and the people of Yucatan have given me very precious memories and an unforgettable education. I cannot keep this all to myself; I want to share these experiences. I only hope that I write sufficiently to arouse your curiosity about this place and encourage you to visit it and be touched by the people, its history, its charm, and its near magical existence. I hope also that my grandchildren will understand why "Tata" choose to live in this foreign land.

I know that there are hundreds if not thousands of books written about Yucatán and the Maya on the shelves. Many, if not all of the books, it seems to me, deal with the Europeans' discovery of the ancient cities in the jungle, scholarly works on the ancient Maya who in their heyday (the Maya, not the scholars) were the most advanced civilization on the planet, or postulating on how and why the civilization met its decline and demise.

I, on the other hand, want you to know the Yucatán of today, which is primarily its people, especially the Maya. In this small book I try to share some of the very special people with you and some of the wonderful experiences that I have been privileged to have.

Thank You

Over the years there has been a small but loyal group of friends who encouraged me to write about my experiences in Yucatán and Mexico and who genuinely understood my unusual, if not caustic, sense of humor and my cartoon view of the world. They understood, too, that beneath it all I enjoy a passion for people and life. You all know who you are. I deeply appreciate your encouragement and support.

I need to thank Sonia Lu Trujillo, the first Yucateca whom I ever met and whose openness and grace enticed me to visit her homeland. Also, Larisa Peniche, who, upon meeting me, told me that, in my heart, I was Yucateco. Thank you also needs to go to Jim Schulze and Lisa Rock for facilitating my entry and continued visits to the Maya village of Tinum where I developed my keen sense of appreciation for these wonderful people. Of these people, I need to single out the Poot Canul family, especially Doña Piedad, for showing me the heart and soul of the Maya, not to mention the wonderful meals that she and daughter Chava prepared me! I also need to thank the people of another Maya village, Seye, that in recent years have taken me into their village and into their hearts.

This could not be done without the wonderful help of Carol Van Klompenburg and the staff at The Write Place. Thank you all so much.

Thank you, too, to Juan Torres and Marissa Perez not only for being dear friends over the years, but also for sharing the beach house, where I was secluded and where this work began to take form and flow. Thank you to my ever patient wife Donna, who took time out of her hectic schedule to read and re-read my rants and ravings. Her work showed clearly that when it came to grammar and spelling, unfortunately, during the early years of my education, there were no special education classes.

1

Aluxes

Did I ever tell you that I have *aluxes* in my house in the city? I am not alone here; faithful Lucy Yah Miam will testify to the same. She has had words with the *aluxes*. Some of them very stern words. OK, for those of you who are asking what the h-e -double hockey sticks is an *alux*, listen up, I'm only telling you this once. An *alux*, pronounced "ah loosh," is a Maya version of the Irish leprechaun and easier to spell. They generally live in the woods, but there has been at least one in my house for years. When I am not there, the *alux* plays tricks on Lucy and scares her. When I am here, the *alux* thinks that it is more fun to mess up my computer. It has messed with every computer that I have had down here. I am using the fifth computer down here; the first four got *aluxed* beyond repair. This year the *alux* is venturing out and changes the wiring between the VHS and DVD players and the televisions both upstairs and down when I am not looking. I have had to rewire the configurations three times since I have been down here. The *alux* also makes sounds. When I put the A/C on, the *alux* makes the sound of the doorbell ringing, and I am constantly running downstairs to find no one at the door. In one floor fan, the *alux* makes the sound of a violin, and in another there are the sounds of soft voices singing.

Nearly all the Maya I know, regardless of education level or social awareness, believe in the *aluxes* and talk freely about them.

Honestly, this is all true, and if you don't believe me you can ask my psychiatrist!

A Day at the Beach

Today I am a Mexican citizen, sort of, and I am still sorting out my rights and responsibilities. "Sort of" means that I still need to renew my status annually for five years before I can apply for permanent status. No, I have not renounced my American citizenship. However, if we invade Iran or Granada again or elect another president named after a plant, I probably will.

During the application process, I could choose a status like "retired." I chose "Independent Teacher," which then allows me to work for the same miserably low wages that everyone else gets here. Well, not everyone is getting a wage, just the lucky ones. Each state or region in Mexico has its own minimum wage. In Yucatan the minimum wage is about $3.80 per DAY, not per hour! That's roughly $7,600 per year, if one is fully employed, which does not happen often. Some things are cheaper here, but not that much cheaper. That's not going to feed a whole family. It creates a whole lot of poor folks. That and the loss of jobs thanks to NAFTA, and it is easy to understand why they are crossing the border (and unfortunately dying) in Arizona.

I am celebrating my new status by preparing to spend a week alone at a friend's beach house on the gulf coast. For a few hours the owner's family is with me. I begin my stay by watching a seven-year-old girl con the living be-jeepers out of her four-year old-sister in a game of gin rummy by changing the rules about every other draw from the pile to suit her needs. Pretty soon, the four year old figures it out and we all get an earful of her frustration and hurt that her best friend and sister is not being trustworthy. Her voice reminded me of Ethel Merman, who could fill any concert hall with her voice without a microphone. Unfortunately, for this performance I had a front row seat; I would have preferred the balcony.

I am the middle of three children myself so I have experienced the con game from both sides. For these two, they are no different than seven- and four-year-olds in Ohio. They are not old enough to have developed cultural differences; they are just children like children anywhere. One thing that I notice often about the children here is that so many of them are terminally cute. The third child in this family is only two months old. His mother has assured me that he is now and will always be the *xtup*. An *xtup* (esh toop) is the youngest member in the family. When he is old enough, his sisters will tease him by telling him that *xtup* is a Maya word and means *estúpido*! His needs are simple. You can feed me, change my diaper, let me sleep on you shoulder but don't ever consider putting me down!

Mom and Grandma are here also. We all seem to be involved in some type of surrogate role. Grandma lost her husband three weeks ago following a five-year illness. Mom lost her husband this week to a convention in Chicago three days ago. My family is in another country. I am trying to remember how long I have known this family, at least fifteen years.

My hosts have returned to the city now, and I have a three-bedroom, three-bath beach house to myself. The front and back of the house are open so that the salty breezes off of the gulf waters blow gently through the house, sometimes a little more than gently! I clearly see and hear each wave as it laps up on the shore. Not far down the beach, a rock jetty sticks out a hundred feet or so. It was constructed along with others as an effort to entice Mother Nature to deposit more sand here. Much of the beach was lost to hurricane Gilbert in 1988—not only the sand beaches but the beach houses as well. My friend Helbert lost his beach house that sat on this very spot and eventually rebuilt about fifteen miles east of here. Two years ago his sons Kuko and Juan bought the rubble and land from him and began to construct a new beach house.

The east side of the pier has a lot of sand on the beach. This side, the west side, does not. The locals blame the pier. The engineers say that it is not so. They also get paid to say that it is not so!

The waves are up to a foot or more now. They start out in the morning very calm and don't start to pick up until about noon. Sometime during the night they quiet down again, and you wake up to calm turquoise waters.

I am probably going to go through some kind of withdrawal. This will be the first day in several months that I will not have internet access. I am not sitting in front of my monitor all day wondering why people don't answer my e-mails instantaneously. Obviously those who do answer right away have about as much work to do as I do. It is like quitting smoking or drinking: there is never a good day to start. Today is a really bad day to start. My beloved Chicago White Sox are finally playing some decent baseball and open tonight with a series with defending American league champions, the Detroit Tigers, and the Chicago Luvabulls open the NBA playoffs against the defending champion Miami Heat. Am I going to watch them both over an internet simulcast? Noooooooo! I am going to be on an isolated lonely deserted beach lucky to have running water. This could alter my view of our creator. It just may be that I am as dumb as I look, and she knew it all along when she made me this way.

Maybe I should have brought some friends along to the beach. You know, friends like Johnnie Walker, Jim Beam, Jose Cuervo, or the Bacardi Brothers. Coca Cola light and tomato juice just isn't cutting it.

I arrived in Yucatan about two months ago under the guise of coming down to work on a book. My dear spouse was going to be away all winter and spring studying at the University of Arizona, so why stay in North Carolina when I could be alone in Yucatan and not speak the language….well, not very well. Other than signing a few documents, I have not written one word until today. I have filled my time with—well, not really filled my time but revolved my life around—mundane things like getting a new propane tank on the roof of the house, getting malfunctioning toilets repaired, getting a functioning ATM card from my bank here, covering for my business colleague who is out of the country, and getting ready to host a group of college students in a month. Today I begin to write, that makes it a good day; let us rejoice and be glad in it. The combination of this tranquil environment and having my residency status straightened out has freed my mind to relax and be creative. I am thoroughly enjoying the moment.

3

Lucy, I'm Home

I have friends in Yucatán whom I have known for, gosh, twelve to fifteen years, I really don't know. Over those years, every time (I am prone, if not addicted, to exaggeration, but this is true) that I have visited their home, the maid just quit. The lady of the

Jorgito, Lucy, and Cruz—1995

house flits around disorganized, discombobulated, frantically trying to accomplish a simple task like pouring a glass of Coca Cola. She is utterly distraught, the MAID JUST QUIT! I often suspect that there never has been a maid; on the other hand, knowing her, I can understand why she cannot keep a maid if she did have one.

In contrast, Lucy has been with me for fourteen years, basically since the day that we bought the house.

We bought the house on Thanksgiving week 1995. It is a condo, two story, three bedroom, 2½ bath. Everything was white—walls, ceilings, and ceramic tile floors with a one-inch stripe of blue near the ceiling. It was little more than a concrete and ceramic shell. There were no light fixtures, no cabinets, no closets, no shelves, no hot water, no propane gas, and no appliances. Just a tad short of being inhabitable. It did have hammock hooks and working toilets. Thank God for small favors.

The following day, the place we were staying at lost its hot water. We thought that, aw what the heck, we can take cold showers in our own new house. So we took our hammocks and moved right in. (We always carry a hammock with us, don't you?) The next day we untangled ourselves from the hammocks and begin to assess what all needed to be done to the house and considered the logistics of carrying eight ceiling fans on our laps on a bus and other challenges. There was a knock on the door. I don't identify front or back, we only have one door, obviously we have a different set of fire safety codes here. The one here says, not to worry, concrete just doesn't burn very well. Knocking at the door was a petite Maya female. She appeared too old to be a child, yet too young to be a woman.

I need to digress for a moment because there has not been an opportune time to lay this foundation. There are two things that you need to know about me. One is that I love to go barefoot. The second is that when the decision was made to buy the house, I insisted that despite local custom, I would not engage an indigenous person as a maid and call her *mi muchacha*, my little girl. Believe or not, these two things have a relationship. Let's go back to the door.

The young woman at the door explained the she worked part-time for another family in the condo complex and that she really needed more work and would we hire her as a cleaning lady. She was twenty three years old, divorced from an abusive husband, and had two children, eight and five. Actually her story was more tragic than that, but I will spare you the details. Juxtaposed to my righteous attitude was the reality that hiring her would literally put food on a table for children where there was none. I happened to turn around and notice the floors. My sweaty bare feet were beginning to leave black footprints on the dusty white floors. Surely I could mop the floor every day on my vacations—NOT! "Young lady, we are leaving for the States in the morning and returning in January. Come see us then. You are hired, but you will NEVER be *mi muchacha*, my little girl. ¿*Cómo se llama?* What is your name?"

"Lucy"

So that is how Lucy came into my life. In the early days I paid her to clean my house and to talk to my wife. That wasn't my intention; it just worked out that way. Despite some despicable acts on the part of her ex, Lucy's family and friends did not support her decision to get a divorce. "Silly girl, everybody knows that a bad husband is better than no husband at all!" They also didn't support her commuting into the city every day to work. There was a textile assembly plant in town where she could make considerably less money. When minimum wage is about $3.80 PER DAY, you aren't making enough to put those boys in day care, somebody had to watch those kids, and the family resented it. Lucy had no one to talk to, except my wife. After she "punched in" for the day she and my wife would talk for an hour to an hour and a half. Every day there was conversation, sharing, crying on shoulders and support. On one hand she was a responsible adult woman trying to feed her children; on the other hand, she was emotionally a frightened little girl.

I have wanted from day one to return to the house, fling the door open and in my best Cuban accent and Desi Arnez impersonation proclaim, "Lucy, I'm home!" I know that Lucy would stare at me like I was an idiot, so I have never done it.

Lucy's boys, Cruz and Jorgito, were extremely curious about the *gringos* for whom their mother worked. There was a good probability that they had never seen a *gringo*. Lucy's father feared that the *gringos* would take Lucy to the States and that they would never see her again. The boys wanted to meet the *gringos* so much and find out what we were all about. Lucy asked if it would be permissible to bring them to work with her one day, and we encouraged her to do just that. Let me insert a piece of information: when we asked Lucy what the boys would like for Christmas, the answer was Power Rangers. How they knew about Power Rangers in the village was beyond me, but they knew. Lucy was to bring the boys on her next scheduled work day with us.

That day came and oh, my! At my door were these two little—and I mean little—boys. They had been spit and polished up real gooooood. They had been scrubbed so clean they were shining. Their jet black hair was all slicked back, and they were wearing their best Sunday-go-to-meetin' pants and shirts. ADOR-ABLE! They took to the house like it was Disney World. It was full of things that they had never seen or at least had never been part of their home life. Our house had truly amazing and incredible things in it . . . like stairs. They went running up and down the stairs. What incredible fun! Up and down, up and down. Then, there was the marvel of marvels, the penultimate discovery, flush toilets. Flush the toilets downstairs, and then run up a flush the toilet upstairs, and back down again to repeat the process. Eventually Jorgito tugged at my wife's garment (I could get a lot of points here if I could tell you what she was wearing and where she got it, but, hey, I'm a guy) and asked if he could have a cookie. She told him that we didn't have any cookies, but he insisted and pulled her into the pantry and pointed them out to her. They were Ritz crackers. The word in Spanish is the same for cookie and cracker. She asked them if they wanted some peanut butter on the crackers. She got a blank look like she had just asked them the square root of fifty seven. They didn't know peanut butter. They knew Power Rangers, but had never heard of peanut butter. Go figure! So with peanut butter crackers in hand, literally, they went back to racing around the house and up and down the stairs with Lucy close behind picking up cracker crumbs off the floor she had just cleaned. We took them to lunch at a Burger King. Just like the peanut butter, these Power Ranger addicts had never had a French fry or a cheeseburger. It was a day that they would remember for a long time. I have.

The pantry early on was an unspoken bone of contention with Lucy, primarily because I was in conflict with local custom. When a house like mine is built here, the sleeping quarters are upstairs and the living quarters are downstairs. Behind the kitch-en is a small room with a sink. Behind that is a smaller room with a toilet and a shower. This is commonly referred to as the *cuarto de servicio*, the MAID'S room. Often the maid is a live–in and that is her space. What I notice about people who have a live-ins is that they can go on about their lives oblivious that there is another person in the house or in the room. When they want something, they just call out the maid's name, and the maid comes a-running.

To me, it's like calling the dog. I'm sorry, I just can't have someone in my house and not feel an obligation to entertain them, to accommodate them, to relate to them. That room cannot be a *cuarto de servicio*; it needs to be a pantry! In the beginning, Lucy, understandably, took a sense of ownership in the space in question. Personal things began to show up. She hung a hammock on the hooks. I wondered if she was slowly trying to move in and not commute back to dirt floors and thatch roofs of her village every night. Meanwhile, I was doing my own subtle things to define the space. First I put in a plastic shelf unit and placed a box of cereal and a supply of napkins on it. Clearly, this was a pantry. Next, I put a small set of plastic drawers on wheels in the corner. I had no idea what I would put in it, but clearly it was pantry furniture. This game went on for about a year or two, and then one day I had a washer and dryer installed in the room. The next day the hammock was gone. I won! I won! I won! I'm sorry, that was childish of me. (But I did win.)

One day Lucy asked if we would like to attend the end of school celebration in her village. You don't come down here and "do" Yucatán. You must come down here and let Yucatán "do" you and part of that is never saying "no" unless the activity is illegal. The last day of school arrives and we (this we is me and my lovely sweet wife, Donna, but this is my story and I try to keep her name out of it) drive to Lucy's village of Seyé. It is pronounced "say yea!" I have taught Lucy to say "yea" when we enter her village. We arrived at Lucy's parents hut and there are the boys, all spiffed up and raring to go. They are fascinated by the car. It's peanut butter time all over again. They all pile in the car and off we go to the school, the boys riding in a car like they were royalty. Two minutes later we arrive at the school; it is a small village. We entered the outdoor play area where Lucy introduced us to the headmaster, her former teacher. Now Seyé is not a drive-through village, you don't through Seyé to get anywhere else. You get off the Merida-Cancun highway and drive about five miles into the henequen fields to get to Seyé, turn around and drive back out. My hair is variegated red and white, my wife is blond, and we are both quite tall in comparison to the villagers. We are a physical phenomenon here. The headmaster invites us to sit at the head table with the mayor's wife. We decline and say that we will be sitting in the back with Grandma. She insists that our presence has honored the village and we must sit in a place of honor for the ceremony. Remember the "don't say no" thing?

We are seated at the table of honor with the mayor's wife. There are about three hundred children running about, grades one through six. They are trying to get this show on the road. This ranks about one notch below trying to organize and lead a university faculty. The program starts. It consists of every class, not every grade, but every class coming out dressed in a folkloric costume of some region of Mexico and doing that region's folk-loric dance. It was all absolutely charming and remarkably well done. One class did a dance that traditionally is accompanied with fireworks. They compensated for that by throwing paper replicas of firecrackers in the air. All the pre-school brothers and sisters went diving on the ground collecting the paper firecrack-ers. Then, it was time for the finale, the dance of the graduating sixth graders. Just then it began to rain, not hard, just a drizzle. Lucy came up from behind and whispered that since her boys had already danced, that we could leave rather than sit in the rain. I responded that as long as the mayor's wife and others stayed, I was staying. The drizzle began to let up and here comes the sixth grade. No folkloric costumes here. The girls came out in ball gowns and all made up with cosmetics and jewelry. These were no little girls; they looked like nineteen-year-old debutantes. The boys came out looking like absolute gentlemen in their tuxedos sans jacket. The music started and they began to dance....the WALTZ! They were performing the Graduation Waltz right here in the middle of nowhere! The beauty of the moment is so strong in my memory that it brings tears to my eyes just remembering it. Feel free to cry with me.

The dancing stopped and the headmaster put a pile of diplomas on the table in front of us. We had a front row seat to the action. Wrong! We were the action. They were calling out the names of the graduates and having my wife and I hand out the diplomas, congratulate the students, and then have their picture taken with us. These poor kids, for the rest of their lives they will have a memory of their graduation with some unknown *gringo* in the photo. In time we were all out diplomas and children and set about to leave. As we were leaving, a little boy came up and said that he was sorry that we couldn't leave the head table and get some fireworks and gave us half of his collection! Those cheap and now old paper fireworks still stand in a vase in my home. Excuse me, it's time to deal with a tear or two; join me if you wish.

Lucy and I have a give-and-take relationship. If I tease her, she teases me back double. She has never been one bit intimidated by me, my career titles, my size, my nothing! She knows that I say outrageous things just to mess with her. One day I got tired of trying to make decent toast in a toaster oven (I have never seen this in the States, but here I have a combination toaster oven/microwave), so I broke down and went out and bought a $9.99 real toaster. Lucy was intrigued with the new appliance, as she is with all the gadgets we have introduced her to. I began the explanation by saying that this was no more than a larger version of a light bulb in a metal box instead of glass. She gave me a look that said, "Don't start with me, fat man; I'm not buying any of this!" By the time I finished explaining how the filaments get hot and burn the bread just like they get hot in a light bulb and would burn your fingers, she thought that just maybe I wasn't the dumbest person that she had ever met. But this isn't about toasters. It's about Lucy's intelligence, orange juice, and curtains.

My sweet wife likes fresh orange juice. Me, I could suck on a can of frozen Minute Maid like a Popsicle, I don't care. We can buy oranges on the street 100 for 200 pesos which is a little less than two cents an orange. She prefers fresh and also likes to get up at Oh my God in the morning. So while I am still sleeping in, she squeezes off a few in the electric squeezer, GRRRRRRRRRR until she has a glassful. It only takes one GR-RRRRRR and I am no longer sleeping in. While we were out one day, Lucy was putting away dry dishes and electric orange juice squeezer parts. When she put the juicer together it made a slight GRR and bingo, Lucy knew how to use the juicer. When we got home Lucy had squeezed all 200 oranges and filled every container in the house. She had saved my wife all that work and me all those early morning GRRRRRRRRRRs! God love her.

My sweet one had made some curtains for the bedroom windows. The windows are double jalousie windows so I brought down double sets of single window rods to install. I started on the outside and the drilling went well. I started to drill the inside and with all my weight and a drill that would go through concrete, I could not penetrate that wall. I ran down to a local store to see if I could find double-wide rods and as luck would have it, they had them in stock. I bought them and brought them home, but I did not have time to install them because we had a date for pizza with friends. During pizza, I shared the curtain rod story. The next morning we left town for a few days in another Maya village. When we returned, I carried my stuff up to the bedroom and to my wonderment all the rods were installed and the curtains were hung perfectly level with all the panels matching perfectly. Our friends Juan and Marissa were the only people who knew about this. Just then the doorbell rang and it was Lucy. "Lucy, when did Juan come over and hang the curtains?"

"He didn't, I did. I thought that since I could figure out how to use the electric juicer that I could figure out how to use Don Alan's drill. I had trouble climbing the ladder in my skirt and then I remembered that I was alone so I just hiked up my skirt and drilled. I used Don Alan's first hole as my guide. I made a mistake on my first hole but you will never find it because I used some of that white stuff you had up there (spackling). The first window took me an hour but after that one, the other one took only fifteen minutes. "

I am beginning to think that this is no ordinary villager.

A couple of years later we were invited once again to the end of the school year celebration. Since our last visit to the school they had constructed an outdoor stage with a roof over it. We, with friends from Texas, were able to avoid celebrity status and took positions in the back where we could move around some with our cameras. The routine was pretty much the same with all the folkloric costumes and dances. The children as always were adorable. This year the sixth grade graduates did the traditional

Yucatecan folk dance, the *jarana*. The girls were beautiful in their multi-layered white dresses and under skirts, all trimmed in embroidered bright colors. The boys stood straight and tall (Kinda. "Tall" really isn't an option for a Maya.) with their white hats, white trousers, and white guayaberra shirts. They wore the traditional Yucatecan sandals. It was quite a scene, a field of white with brilliant colors swirling all about. As it turns out, not every sixth grader was dancing. One little girl had been in an automobile accident and was not yet able to walk. They dressed her up in a pretty little white party dress, put her in a plastic chair, carried her out, and sat her at center stage. The finale of this event was to be a releasing of doves. Now, I don't know why people do this. Some people seem to think that it is a beautiful thing to release a dove, that it symbolizes something good. Well, symbolize this, bird-brains! Why don't you try to impress me by not capturing those helpless little birds in the first place! The graduates were to get their doves at the end of the dancing and on cue, away they go. The idea for the little girl in the chair was to have her hold her dove throughout the dance. Bad idea. The dove naturally tried to escape its captivity. The harder the dove worked at freedom from the little girl's brown fingers, the tighter her little brown fingers clutched the dove.

For every action there is a reaction. Einstein and I worked that out. The reaction of the dove to being squeezed was to become smaller by releasing excrement all over the front of the little girl's white party dress. Oh! Please don't look down, sweetheart. Lucy and my wife are sick people. They thought that the sight of a bird crapping all over a little crippled girl was hilarious. They were doubled over with laughter, creating a minor scene, a disturbance, if you will, in the back of the audience. My friends from Texas and I slowly moved away not wanting to be associated with this demented *gringa* and her Maya friend. The moment had come for the release. On cue, the graduates, with all their energy, hurled the doves into the air and into the roof, knocking the doves silly. They then came tumbling back to earth to be immediately scooped up and swept away by the younger boys. Thank you, Lucy, for the invitation to the first annual "Maiming of the Doves" ceremony in Seyé, Yucatán!

There are so many wonderful memories of Lucy. One day I came home and my little patio garden was completely torn apart, plants uprooted, pots moved all over. Lucy had seen a snake and was trying to find it and kill it before it got into the house. She never did find the snake. I suspect the snake saw her coming and got out of there as fast as possible. She assumes full authority for the plants and garden because it is obvious to her that I don't know beans about plants. In comparison to her life, we have so many decorative items. Sometimes she spends as much time rearranging things as she does cleaning. She rearranged my desk . . . once!

Lucy eventually remarried and had a third son, Angel. I remember, as an honored guest at Angel's baptism party, I got to sit directly in front of the eight foot loud speaker. The word "loud" does not do justice to the sound coming out of it. I begged the boys to give me a tour of the property just to get away. "So, that's a chicken. I have always wondered what they looked like. Got any more like that around here? I sure would like to see them." Not too recently, Lucy invited me and some friends to a novena. She had converted her home into a chapel and it was full of friends and family giving thanks. What I remember most about that day was that every time I pulled out my camera to take a shot, her nursing sister pulled out her breast to feed the baby. I owe you one for that, Lucy. I also remember visiting her late grandfather's home after a hurricane hit it.

Cruz is in college now, and Jorgito is in high school! Cruz will be 21 this year and is in the second year of a university degree program in computers. Jorgito plays sports and is a very bright young man, but hasn't set any career goals for himself yet. Angel is a real cutie and is nine years old! This is all hard to believe since it was just yesterday that they had never had peanut butter or a French fry.

Each year, as my Spanish improved a little, Lucy and I would communicate more. We began to share more of our lives and were able to give more support to each other. She was never my maid, but was the woman who cleaned my house. I think that is more respectful to her. But now, she isn't the woman who cleans my house, she is more of a house manager. We make decisions about the house together, and sometimes she initiates ideas. I used to run around trying to find electricians and plumbers; now Lucy does all of that. She has grown and matured so much from that frightened young woman I met in 1995. In a way I feel like Lucy and I have been growing older together. She is a mature, intelligent, competent, delightful woman, and a great mom. Best of all . . . she is my friend.

 **4**

December 2001

T he sun sets early in December in Yucatán so that by five in the afternoon the lights of Merida sparkle as far as the eye can see.

The landing pattern took a northerly route and as the pilot tilted the plane, I could see the decorations on the Paseo Montejo, the fountain on the Paseo lit for the holidays, Gran Chapur department store wrapped like a present, and even my house.

I had not yet unpacked when ten or so children began serenading me outside my door. So beautiful were their faces, eyes, smiles, and voices.

Ana Cristina, my first Yucatecan grandchild, not yet two, called out *"Tata, Tata, venga y baila"* to the tune on the radio.

I started on a new adventure, traveling to Punta Allen with the bridge out at Boca Paila. A great time was had with very special, if not poco loco, friends.

The waiter from Capitan Marisco rushed to greet me as I began my daily ritual of walking the beach or power walks at the Ceiba pool. I met Donna from Canada on that walk and soon sent her on her way down the road to visit the poco locos at Punta Allen.

A two-hour breakfast with Blanca was not sufficient to share all that happened in our lives the last four months. It seems like every time we are together is special.

Tuesdays and Thursdays are still *intercambios* with Luchi. It always gives us both an opportunity to reflect on the truly important things in our lives. Maybe we learn a little of each other's language too!

Ramon, Jorge, Adrian, Eric, and the one I can never remember take turns hugging me at Portico Peregrino. The other clients are puzzled by all the affection and references to past jokes and pranks between us.

Cuman, the little three-year-old Chinese Yucateco, watches me unload my computer, and he proudly tells me that he has a computer and knows how to use it. I believe that it is the first time I have ever heard him speak.

Carin was shouting *"mira,* Alan, *mira"* as she came running up with her new brown furry puppy named Danesa.

The children giggled with glee as they watched my dancing Santa Claus, the latest addition to my deliberately tacky Christmas decorations.

Each and all seemed so different to the eye, but to the heart there was a strong common thread . . . "Alan, welcome home this December 2001."

5

The Pork Chop

What can be said about a pork chop? Let's find out together! I will try to stay with the subject at hand and not be clever by making references to, for example, Pork Chop Hill, a battlefield in some war gone by. I wasn't there and am thankful for that.

I was, however, in Iowa for seven long-suffering years that seemed a lifetime. Occasionally it was twenty-six degrees below zero in Iowa, and days took a long time to roll over into another day. At twenty-six degrees below zero even time slows down. Iowa at that time was, if not close to being, the porcine capital of America. Personally I was not involved in the porcine world, breeding and peddling and such, but on some days when the winds shifted towards town, it was unavoidable to deal with the reality that I was in the middle of a state full of pigs. Even when it wasn't twenty six-degrees below zero, one had a tendency to stay indoors to avoid the pungent odors of pig *xix* (pronounced "sheeeesh" and meaning "that which is left" in Maya.....you can have *xix* in a bowl of mashed potatoes without an issue, but when pigs leave *xix* around the barn yard, it changes your world!) All of this is to say that when it comes to things porcine, pigs, ham, bacon and pork chops . . . we've met!

In 1989 I made my first trip to a foreign country, not technically true, having been to Canada on several visits since I was twelve. I don't consider Canada a foreign country; to me it is just another Michigan or Minnesota but without the graffiti and litter. An exception is made, of course, for Montreal, which also doesn't have graffiti and litter, but unlike the majority of us on this continent, its citizens have not gotten over the fact that they came from somewhere else and have a need to speak a foreign language. I am not hung up on the language thing as much as I am that Montreal lost a major league baseball team out of utter neglect. That's un-American, just like Los Angeles not being able to keep a professional football team because they just don't care. Understandably, I don't consider Los Angeles an American city either.

Lest I digress, in 1989 I left the U. S. of A. for Mexico for the first time, well, not counting the time I walked over to Nogales, Senora, looking for a bargain on a pair of black cowboy boots. Found some interesting barrios on that little walk. In 1989 it was twenty-six degrees below zero in Iowa, had been for a few days, and looked like it was going to be that was for the foreseeable future. Mexico was the warmest option that I had where someone else would pay the airfare and also had the responsibility to find a car that would start in twenty-six degrees below zero and get me to the airport. (Pig *xix* is no longer an issue at twenty-six degrees below zero!) I could have gone just about anywhere but warm seemed like a good idea.

We arrived safely in Merida, Yucatán, Mexico, we being my spouse and myself. I basically spoke no Spanish, having the consistency to have failed Spanish in both high school and college, save a few essential words like cerveza and taco. My spouse had a Ph.D. in Spanish; she came in handy.

It was eighty-five degrees, sunny with a breeze in Merida. My body thought I had died and gone to heaven. We walked over to a little park to imbibe a national beverage and listen to some live marimba music. Don't like live marimba music? Iowa and twenty-six degrees below zero are ready when you are! I would have listened to a live concert of Zamfir and his pan flute to avoid Iowa. Just then someone called out my name. There was actually someone in that little park that I knew, and they knew me! I was beginning to get comfortable!

Later we went over to a little place named Portico del Peregrino, literally "gate of the wanderer," for a bite to eat. We walked through the gated archway, down a little hallway, and into an open courtyard filled with plants, tables, and chairs. There were a couple of side rooms that were air conditioned for summer use when the temperatures got between "are you kidding me" and "I think that I'm going to die."

I quickly learned from the menu that in Yucatán one cannot find anything resembling menu items at Taco Bell, Chi Chi's, Nacho Mama's, or any other Mexican restaurant in the U. S. of A. My vague recollection is that I played the good tourist and didn't search the menu for a hamburger (or a pork chop) and tried a local delicacy like *pollo de mole*, which is wonderful. Somewhere I had picked up the notion that the Mexican version of American meats was generally the thickness and consistency of shoe leather. The food and the great attention of the staff made me vow to return to Portico del Peregrino, home of my first meal in Mexico.

Nearly twenty years later I still have my first meal of my visit to Yucatán at Portico del Peregrino and often my last one. That probably makes about sixty meals by now. Over the years the same staff is there and they as well as the owner have become close to us, like family. They worry about me when I don't come for a period of time. We always spend some pre-meal time catching up on each other's lives. My Spanish has improved to a notch above just smiling and nodding my head. We laugh, hug, and are always genuinely glad to see each other. I have learned the art of a good three-hour lunch to break the habits of my daily life U. S. of A. and transition into the slower gentler cycles of Yucatán.

One time early on, I did try the pork chop and it was the best, juiciest pork chop I had ever eaten. They always serve the chops (big ones too) with apples, just simple old apples but prepared in a way that makes them the best apples I have ever tasted. So for years now, I don't travel to a foreign country with a foreign language with foreign ways. I travel back to Portico del Peregrino a comfort place with comfort food and comfort people. After three or four or more hours at lunch, I successfully make the transition to fully enjoy these people and this land.

I keep coming back to this enchanted land and its wonderful people. Why? Never underestimate the power of a good pork chop!

6

Don Luis

I stand by my claim that Yucatán happens to you, if you allow it. Over the nearly twenty years that I have been sojourning in Yucatán, every visit has had an unplanned occurrence that left a warm and special memory. This time it was meeting Don Luis.

We have an unritual here (an unritual is something that we repeatedly don't do), and it is that we don't cook for two. At the end of our first day this particular visit, we chose Tango Gaucho as the restaurant for the evening. The choice is a simple one. Tango Gaucho is less than a block from our house, the owners are friends of ours, and the food is terrific! The cuisine is Argentine, but what sets it apart is that our friend Mariel makes her own sauces for all the dishes as well as the pastries and empanadas. Our friend Horacio makes his own processed meats and sausages.

We arrive, as usual, earlier than the rest of Yucatán. We just can't seem to get our body clocks set for a nine or ten p.m. dinner. The restaurant is in an old colonial style home, where Horacio and Mariel live upstairs. Tango music gently flows from room to room. The walls are still a gentle green and yellow with Mariel's portraits and other artwork decorating them. We take our usual table and the waiter displays his sharp memory by asking about Frank and still chuckles that we named a little female kitten Frank Thomas, The Big Hurt, the 2nd. At any moment we expect Mariel and Horacio to come in, sit down, and chat for a while catching up on all the news in each other's lives.

They do arrive, but insist that we sit at a larger table in the next room. The four of us are joined by an elderly man wearing a warm smile. The waiter brought our drinks; we did not order them, he just remembers. Normally there is a serving of empanadas *en la casa*, on the house. They come and while I am trying to recall which shape is which kind of empanada, *carne, espinaca,* or *elote,* meat-spinach or corn, more unordered food arrives. Horacio's special thinly sliced cold meats, cheeses, hearts of palm in a cream based sauce, olives, grilled onions and tomatoes, and more. We ordered our main dish for the evening, my friends from Texas, of all places, rave that the *churrasco* here is the finest beef they have ever eaten. Mariel's pastas, enriched with her special sauces, are out of this world. I chose a chicken in a four cheese sauce with specific instructions to the waiter that it be defeathered before it comes to the table. He will remember that the next time we go!

We toast the day, and a special nod for those not with us, and begin to chat. We finally hear from the elderly man.

He is Don Luis. Calling him Don means that he is elderly and respected. He has been a deeply loved father figure for Horacio for a long time. He is eighty-five years old and remembers when dirt was born. A deep tan covers him, maybe from all the years aboard ship. He jokes that after all his years working in forty-meter-deep water, they now have him on a project in one-and-a-half meters deep! There is a science exploration ship up on the coast studying the Chicxulub crater and the effect the Chicxulub meteor had on the shallow coast of Yucatán. A Greenpeace ship is harassing it because they believe that the exploration is doing harm to the gulf floor. Somehow Don Luis is in the middle of the dialogue. His Spanish invokes a phrase that I hear often in North Carolina, "You aren't from around here, are you?"

Sometime before the main dishes arrive the children of Mariel and Horacio arrive, Claudia and Alejandro, both in their early twenties. The have arrived in time to hear most of Don Luis's stories.

Don Luis is not from Yucatán; he is Argentine, as are Mariel and Horacio and the children. They have all traveled a long way from home to be together again. Despite pre-dating dirt, Don Luis is strong and healthy, his mind is quick, and his eyes twinkle. There is a gentle strength about him and a demeanor that assures you that you can believe every word that he utters. He enjoys a good laugh and he smiles a lot, possibly because his memories are crisp and clear and full of warmth and adventure.

Some of his memories are of being on land, especially in the United States. His favorite place was Texas. He taught Oceanography at Texas A&M back when it was still a college. He possibly was there when Bear Bryant began football coaching career at A&M before becoming a legend at Alabama. I didn't ask. I also didn't ask where they did Oceanography lab work in land-locked College Station, Texas! He remembers fondly and misses the music of Texas—the honky-tonk music and the dancing. An Argentine would embrace a culture that dances.

He laughs when reminiscing the time at Woods Hole, Massachusetts, they were putting a research vessel out of service. Don Luis asked them to donate the ship to Argentina for research. Politics and regulation prohibited them from giving the ship away so they made him buy it, for a dollar! He is currently negotiating another $1 a ship deal.

The teacher in him appeared when he told us all about the British explorer, Shackleton. No one would leave the table that evening without knowing why Shackleton was the greatest explorer of all. He showered him with praises and accolades. He recalls that Shackleton, with several shipwrecks in the iceberg-filled waters between Argentina and Antarctica, never lost a crewmember. He always went back repeatedly, if need be, to save his shipwrecked and stranded crews. Don Luis knows these stories first hand from his many years at sea in the Argentine Navy as captain of an ice breaker. He shared stories of meeting up with, if not rescuing, ships and crew from the USA, England, Germany, and many other countries.

I learned later that Don Luis has been honored by NASA and was the first Latin American to earn a Ph.D. in Oceanography. I never saw him before, and I may never see him again, but he is now in a long list of special memories that I carry from my moments in Yucatán. To top off the evening, our food and drinks were on the house. That night we were family!

7

The Shelf

In all my years in Yucatán I have just had my second occurrence of my Spanish failing me. My first was several years ago trying to get my hair cut, or as they say in Eastern Pennsylvania, "get my hairs cut, yessirree, gonna get all of them cut." In Merida, whenever I got comfortable with someone to work on my coif, they would go out of business. So I found a new place, for me, on the Circuito Colonias not far from my house. The staff was all kind of cute and the clientele all looked OK so I gave it a whirl. The young gal did a nice job on my hair and taught me that *cejas* was the word for eyebrows. She then queried me about the beard. I thought that doing the whole head was a good idea and nodded my head. Somehow, and to this day I still don't know how, we went from a trim to removal mode! She got an inch and a half off one side before my Banshee cries sent her cowering into the corner. The rest of the staff apparently thought that this was a good learning experience for her and let her work this out with me herself. Like Lucy does with the alux, I used some stern words, letting her know that this beard was considerably older than she was. She sheepishly asked if I wanted the other side the same. "Oh, no," I told her, I thought being lopsided for the next four months would be a fashion future statement.

The second occurrence of failure of my limited but pathetic Spanish skills.....wait let's stop and let me explain that I do not consider standing there and looking stupid with someone jabbering away at me in Spanish a failure. I view it as more of a condition. To fail, I actually have to try to speak Spanish. I have found that standing around with a blank look on your face and being frightfully old gets me more than trying to learn a new language at a nursing home age. The second failure came just recently.

On occasion, I have asked the *carpintero* of Seye (Lucy Yah Miam's village) to make things for me out of wood. Makes sense to me, he is a *carpintero*. The routine is that I draw something, explain it to Lucy and she gets an estimate from the *carpintero*. I then make a deposit, and it is ready in a couple of weeks. This time I drew a corner shelf that had five ascending-sized shelves with three legs. This would hold the little stereo system and other things and would tuck nicely behind the old Spanish style folding wooden doors that I also designed and would be out of sight and give me more floor space. I could then also hang the speakers in the patio and really tick off the neighbors, which has been the impetus for this whole project.

I received two proposals from José Timmer (*timmer* being the Dutch word for *carpintero*). For roughly $75, as I understood Lucy, he would make the shelves and assemble them in the corner. However if I put them in the corner (which meant driving to Seye to pick them up), it was only $55. I opted for the $55 pick up option. The following week, Lucy (after a long arduous day of cleaning the house a little, taking two food breaks, and watching a couple of soap operas on the TV) and I climbed aboard the Ol' Family Truckster and set out for Seye and arrived at Lucy's house. Lucy's boys came out of the house carrying five shelves without legs to the truck. Oops, my bad! I am thinking now that the issue was that José Timmer didn't have the size of wood needed for the shelf legs and that I would have to go down to the "*Carpinteros* "R" Us" store and buy some. I am having a funny feeling that in the end this will cost me more than the twenty dollars saved.

Lucy thinks that I can wall mount the shelves, but I am the only one of us who has had a physics course and I think that they are two large for wall mounts. So I went down to our local "*Carpinteros* "R" Us" and bought three 2"x2"x7' pieces of wood, some wood glue, and a dark stain and brush. I went over to the electrical tool department and was chagrined to see that a decent jig saw cost around $200. Right now I am having a rotator cuff problem and hand sawing these things is not an option. I am not ready to turn this into a $300 project! I am pulling one from *Gone with the Wind* and will think about this tomorrow!

Several tomorrows came and went before I borrowed a carpenter who was working at a neighbor's house to make the cuts. I paid him ten dollars for his effort and am now over-spent on the twenty dollar savings. The pieces sat around for a few days before I tried to assemble it. The leg pieces were just crooked enough that they created too much pressure to use wood glue. To nail the shelves together I would need at least four hands. Lucy volunteered that the new plumber/electrician could probably do it. It just so happened that I needed some plumbing work done so Lucy called him. He came over and spent the longest time trying to put it together, the cuts on the back leg were not made correctly and it was a tricky process to make it work. At one point, Lucy called me down to see the progress. She also let me know in no uncertain terms that she thought it was very ugly and that I should reconsider the option of wall mounts. Normally Lucy is right and I give in, but hey, this is my idea, my design, I'm sticking to my guns this time. It really does look like the work of a committee! Over the next weekend, I stained it and that gave it a very different look, almost like an antique. Before Lucy came for another day's work, I filled the shelves. After seeing the finished project, Lucy claims to like it now.

I think she wants a raise.

8

And the Rains Came

It is hot again in Yucatán. They don't use thermometers or cite degrees; it's either paradise or really hot. "How hot?" friends ask me. When I tell them that this time of year it can be 110-114 degrees, they respond, "Oh, a dry heat like Phoenix or Tucson." No, it is not a dry heat. It is 110-114 degrees with the humidity of South Florida or the Gulf Coast of Louisiana. They cannot put those two concepts together.

I grew up with the opposite problem, cold. We had an index that calculated the effect on the body of a real temperature, the wind, and the humidity. We called it the "Wind Chill Factor." When it was actually 25 below zero, the effect on your body with a nice wind and a little humidity was 100 below zero. We were cold . . . to the bone, and my bones never warmed up until June each year. The reverse index is a heat index. Today in North Carolina it was 95 degrees with a 103 degree heat index. We don't use the heat index in Yucatán. We know when it is no longer nice and is now Oh My God hot.

I have seen the devastation and destruction of water from hurricanes; I understand that it is heavy and strong. I generally don't translate that into air. But the air here is heavy and strong. You first feel it when you step off the plane onto the jet way and the air almost knocks you down. You labor to walk the jet way to claim your luggage and go through the unique Yucatán customs. You breathe slower and deeper, forcing yourself through the air. The hot heavy air also penetrates to the bone, exacting all of your energy in a brief amount of time. Wherever you are going, you want to get there quickly and sit or lie down.

It hasn't rained for six months. It often goes six months without rain despite all the moisture in the air. The dry plants and ground are perfect for the slash and burn agricultural practiced over thousands of years by the indigenous Maya. The crops were planted when the sun forms a shadow of a snake going down the side of the temple Kukulcan at the ancient city of Chichen Itza . . . the spring solstice. The sun and the temple are accurate every year on the spring solstice without needing a leap year to adjust to the earth and stars. Remarkable architects and astronomers, those Maya!

In recent days, the indigenous farmers have been doing *novenas*. Drinking, eating, and praying for nine days for the rains to come. The ninth day is the festival of San Juan.

The six months without rain and then the arrival of tropical rains make this place a combination of a semi-arid tropical landscape. We have cactus and palm trees growing side by side. Just one example of the many seemingly antithetical phenomena of the place. Now, the crops are nearly failed and you cannot conceive of another day in the unbearable heat and humidity. You curse the heat. You take multiple showers trying to get relief. Relief can be found at the beach and lasts until the tropical sun has burned you into pain or you leave the beach and lose the breeze that has made it feel twenty degrees cooler. The day at the beach is over, the last day of the festival of San Juan is over, and then the rains came.

The drops are big at first and wide apart. They splatter on the dry dusty ground and pavements spewing little showers of dirt and water barely blended together. Slowly the drops get bigger and closer together until they join into a solid sheet of water, sheet after sheet brought by cool winds and washing the parched earth until you can smell the dirt again. Your spirits and body are refreshed nearly instantly.

The downpour lasts normally no more than thirty minutes. It stops suddenly. Everything smells clean, water stands all about, and where there is land and pavement above the water, a thin vapor arises. The sun pops out, and it is surreal for about ten minutes. In thirty minutes it will be beastly hot again, but you have been refreshed, and you know the rains will come again and that you can make it through another day.

The rainy season has started, June 13th this year, and every afternoon about four o'clock, just when the siestas and extra showers weren't enough to get relief from the heavy heat, the rains came, once again. We know that we can make it until the fall as long as the rains come. In the fall, our paradise returns.

Maybe it is because I am a year older and a year further out of shape, but I find myself needing more time to adjust to the heat and humidity. It used to take three days or so, but now I need four or five days to adjust. It makes me even more grateful when the rains come.

9

To my friends from
Turtle Time

ortugear or no *Tortugear*, That is the Question!
    "Once upon a time" began many an old time story when stories started at the beginning and finished at the ending. All the stories, in good time, came to an end.

There is nothing quicker than a New York minute, and it is nearly over before it begins, hardly worth the experience.

Either war or peacetime is constantly with us. We cannot escape them. Wartime usually begins much quicker than peacetime, but they both eventually run their course.

The longest and shortest times are one and the same, the two-minute warning. It all depends on if you are winning or losing.

Children today occasionally need a timeout. So do adults, but there is no need to impose it on them. Timeouts feel like an eternity but rarely last for more than a few minutes.

Twilight time can be a special time of the day, good for romance or reflection. It can also be the special time just before the last night falls, never to return.

Quality time happens when two or more are real, able to give and receive. It builds relationships and goes on until interrupted by the minutia of life.

Real time is a contemporary buzzword that means that I am actively interacting with something/someone here to fore technologically impossible to accomplish.

Unreal time is actually a real time but with experiences beyond our expectations. Real time and unreal time have short lives.

Turtle time is an altogether different time. It can happen anywhere at anytime. Everyone in turtle time has validity and what can occur during turtle time has no boundaries. Turtle time has no fixed duration and, in fact, once started, could go on forever, suspended occasionally by a short night's sleep or a siesta.

Other times are free and available to all, but there are entry requirements to turtle time. Turtle time requires a good drink, a good friend, and a free mind. We are heavy laden with the responsibilities of getting through this life; turtle time gives us the focus, spirit, and energy to live it with joy.

June 2002

*Turtle time is a play on words with friends in Mexico using *Tortuga* (turtle) for *Tertulia* (an intellectual discussion group in Spain)

✺ 10 ✺

Tinum

Tinum is an indigenous Maya village of, I dunno, maybe 5,000 people located about thirty minutes north and east of the ruins of the great ancient Maya city of Chichen Itza. It is on the road between Izamal and Valladolid, for those of you who may have had an Avon or Fuller Brush route in that region of the world. In another story or two, I have mentioned Doña Piedad; this is her village.

Maybe about 1990 (I don't do dates well, it brings about memories about old girl friends and the like) a clock salesman went through Tinum and did very well unloading a lot of clocks to the villagers. Soon after, a group of college professors from a small college in Iowa were in Tinum on a grant to "Internationalize" them. They were doing whatever faculty do when they go abroad and are able to use things like toothpaste as a tax deduction. They were trying to adjust to sleeping in a hammock under juana thatch, and wondering just what kind of critters were running around in the rafters. (I was in Punta Allen once with friends and an iguana fell from the rafters and landed on a friend's chest. I don't know who was more startled, my friend or the iguana.) Back to the American faculty; their biggest problem in getting to sleep, however, was that the clocks chimed every hour on the hour and then played a computerized old American song like "She'll be Comin' 'Round the Mountain" or "Oh Susanna." Of course, every clock was set to a slightly different time so that the song heard in the hut could be heard repeated in the neighboring huts for a several minutes after every hour. The faculty pretty much stayed awake all night in anticipation of the next American classic to be emanating from the village clocks. I wasn't there but my sweet wife was, and she shared the story with me, and it served as my first glimpse into village life.

No story about Tinum would be complete without mentioning "Crazy" Robert and Doña Betina. I think that he is called "Crazy Robert" now not because he was considered crazy, but rather to differentiate him from Robert the Younger who occasionally visits the village now-a-days and may not be quite as "unique" as Crazy Robert. Then again, he could have been crazy. I never met him, and I am just giving him the benefit of the doubt. As I understand the history, "Crazy" Robert bought some land in Tinum next to Don Adolfo and built a house, or bought an already built house on some land next to Don Adolfo, who cares, it's not important. We just need to know that "Crazy" Robert was in Tinum next door to Don Adolfo; actually, being next door to Don Adolfo may not be all that important either. *Ni modos*, whatever! Watch out! Here comes a digression. By the time that I started to visit Tinum, Don Adolfo was in his eighties and no longer there, but living in the city of Valladolid with relatives in his later years. I met him in Valladolid soon after my full hip replacement. (Hey Doc, could we save a little money and put in only half a hip? Never happens!) I was using a beautiful cane, hand carved in Mexico, for assistance that I had purchased on South Street in Philly. Don Adolfo thought that my one-of-a-kind cane was a tad more attractive, not to mention more macho, that the sawed off broom handle that he was using. He wanted to trade canes straight up, but I was insisting on the broom handle and two village maidens. We resolved the impasse with my promise that when I no longer needed the cane, it would be his. A few months later, at Christmastime, I went back to Valladolid and presented Don Adolfo with a hand carved Mexican cane adorned with a bright red ribbon. OK, can we get back to Crazy Robert and Doña Betina now?

Doña Betina, an American, met Crazy Robert maybe on a plane flight or somewhere and learned about Tinum, visited, fell in love with Tinum, and built a pretty little stone house on the

other side of Crazy Robert than Don Adolfo. During this time,
I am told, Crazy Robert was more than just disturbed with the
Pentecostal church across the street and their propensity to praise
the baby Jesus with loud rock and roll type songs deep into the
night, even into the early morning. Crazy Robert's solution to the
baby Jesus praising was to run electrical wires out to a cave in
the back of the property where he could sit and read in peace and
quiet during the praise the baby Jesus periods. He doesn't sound
too crazy to me. Another prevalent concept is that he was also ro-
mantically crazy about Doña Betina but that Doña Betina wasn't
all that crazy about Crazy Robert. He was last seen clutching a
broken heart and wandering about Guatemala.

Doña Betina in the meantime began inviting people to visit
her home *Casa Peregrina* (house of the wanderer) to learn about
the life of the Maya. Soon people from all over the world were
visiting Tinum and garnering an appreciation and respect for
these remarkable people. The tradition of Tinum hosting foreign
travelers continues to this day with many of the village families
participating in providing food and lodging and sharing their
lives. By the time that I began visiting Tinum, Doña Betina was in
her eighties and living back in the United States. Friends of mine
had bought Crazy Robert's property and had constructed new *nas*
(huts) and *palapas* to enhance the visitors' experience.

On an early visit, friends were visiting with us during
the holidays. We were hanging out near a small park, and some
elderly men were regaling us with stories about the village.
Tales of the early days were being offered by Don Pepe and Don
Pablo with the translation from Mayan to Spanish being done
by Don Chivo and into English by our friend Lisa. It was a great
introduction into Tinum. Later, after dinner with at a neighbor's
na we walked into the center of town. The center of town was
very traditional for this part of the world. A village, or city for
that matter, has a downtown square. Originally on one side of
the square stood the Catholic church. A second would have the
village or regional government building. A third would often
have the house of the founder, and stores will fill in the remaining spaces. Tinum was traditional. The local Catholic church was

open and we looked in to see the Christmas decorations. This was not a particularly affluent community, although more affluent than many, so the decorations were modest. The nativity scene in the front of the church caught our eye. It was put together with whatever may have been available in the congregation. The stable was understandably a *palapa* rather than the barn-like structure that we normally conjur up. Instead of the bales or containers of hay, the plastic baby Jesus lay in a Maya hammock and was frankly a little large for the size of the manger. He was larger in fact than the smaller plastic Joseph and Mary figures. Someone in the village at one time or another had obtained a Mattel zoo set and the animals, in addition to the traditional cows and sheep, included lions, elephants and giraffes. It was obviously a collaborative effort of the parishioners. The most curious part of the nativity scene was outside of the *palapa*. Just outside of the *palapa* was a replica of a *batea* (a Maya wooden wash basin for laundry). Standing at the *batea*, taller than the rest of the nativity figurines, stood a Barbie doll with her long blonde hair done up in a pony tails and wearing a bandana around her head. Fortunately, I don't have a need to understand everything.

Our group returned to our respective *nas* for the night. We were sleeping at Doña Betina's home for the evening. Before trying to fall asleep for the night, I was thumbing through a guest book where visitors from all over the world had signed in and wrote glowing comments about their experiences. As I turned the pages, I came across a photo of Doña Betina in her youth . . . a tall slender woman with long blonde hair . . . done up in a pony tail and wearing a bandana around her head. She was obviously highly regarded by the villagers, and now I understood the Barbie doll in the nativity scene. It was Betina, an important part of the village in their praising of God for the holidays.

During another visit to Tinum, there was to be a celebration of a new *palapa* (a thatch building without sides) at the home of friends. Our friend Piedad and daughters were bringing the fixings for *panuchos*. Robert the Younger and I had gathered some firewood in the woods to build a fire in the fire pit that had been cut into the *palapa* concrete floor. Doña Piedad and others had

begun the preparations for *panuchos*. To make a *panucho* one needs
many years experience in working with corn meal over an open
fire and making a perfectly sized tortilla without even looking
at it, and enough *masa* (corn meal) to make a four-inch tortilla
on a hot metal griddle called a *comal*. No fair using utensils! One
picks up a hot tortilla and flips it over to cook on the other side
and eventually pulling off the griddle with one's fingers . . . carefully! When cooked, snip the tortilla and blow into it to separate
it, kinda like a pita bread. Now wasn't that easy! Oh, but they still
aren't *panuchos*. One can let these tortillas set around for a while.
When the guests began to get lean and hungry looks about them,
take a tortilla and spread a layer of refried beans on the inside.
Then (utensils allowed for this step) place the tortilla into hot oil
and deep fry until crisp enough to hold toppings, like a tortilla
chip only larger. Remove the tortilla from the hot oil and put
down the utensil. On the top of the tortilla (don't make me mention what happens when you try to put toppings on the bottom
and don't ask me which side is up), place small sliced onion, diced
tomato, some shredded chicken or pork, and top it off with a slice
of avocado. Viola, you have just made your first *panucho*, enjoy!
Robert the Younger ate eighteen *panuchos* that night! That had to
have been some kind of world record!

On that visit to Tinum, I was just off a riveting performance
as Uncle Toby in Shakespeare's *Twelfth Night*. Some nameless
American couple form Iowa had told the villagers of my recent
thespian activities and encouraged them to demand a command
performance as part of the dedication of the new *palapa*. My guess
is that there have been darn few, if any, traveling theatre troupes
traversing the peninsula Yucatán in recent years, especially
Shakespearean specialists, and that the interest from the villagers was simple curiosity as to just what was theatre anyway and
just what does one have to do to do theatre. So, being the accommodating fellow that I am, missing nineteen other cast members,
some scenery like a castle and stuff, and some props, I prepared
to do a shortened monologue version of *Twelfth Night*, in Spanish.
Let me just add that at that time I was nowhere near as fluent in
Spanish as I am now when I use my forty or fifty word vocabu-

lary with utmost confidence. I knew that I needed to use visuals as much as possible to help reduce the language barriers. So, I worked up a sword fight scene with the handsome prince who had his eyes on my buxom niece. I gave myself a crash course on the required vocabulary: sharp (to define my finely honed broom stick), sword, bad, good (I actually already knew bad and good), fight, handsome, etc. With the *panuchos* firmly settled in my stomach, I began to narrate the sword fight, flitting about from tree to tree outside of the *palapa*, occasionally pulling a speaker of English aside and gave instructions to them along the lines of, "when I spit in your face, look shocked and then wave your finger in my face and rebuke me, no spitting back is not rebuking". I darted in and out of the *palapa* chasing and retreating from the prince with my broomstick flailing in the evening air. I think that my success of sharing the marvels of Shakespeare with the villagers was clearly defined when an elder of the village asked a friend of mine, "does this happen to him often?"

Shortly after a heavy dosage of doths and prithees and other Shakespearean lingo, the rapier sharp end of my broomstick came close enough to Robert the Younger that his faithful dog, Jaime interpreted my actions as a threat and with a low growl and all of her pearly whites bared, announced that the play was over. Thus endeth the first and last Annual Shakespeare in the Jungle Festival. Uncle Toby, however, lived to see another day in the village.

During a subsequent visit to Tinum (by the way, are you confusing Tinum with Tulum? A lot of people do that. Not well informed people, but still a lot of people) I learned that the third daughter of Doña Piedad had given birth to a second daughter. Now when Maya children are born it is customary to name them and also nickname them very quickly. Rarely is a Maya family so poor that they cannot afford a really good nickname. It's not like my own family when my brothers and I were born. When we were born we couldn't afford nicknames, so none of have any. It was worse for my older brother who not only was deprived of a nickname, he never got a middle name either. Must have something he said to my mother at birth because my younger brother and I at least have middle names . . . but we paid a price for that. In a cost saving measure, they pulled letters out of our first names. My younger brother John had the "h" pulled out and has spent his whole life (well, not yet) as Jon. It has worked out pretty well for him, and you have to listen real hard to hear the difference in pronunciation. My name, Allen is a fine manly name, but they pulled out the extra and unused "l" AND the "e," repeating the already paid for "a" to make it Alan, a weaker, less prone to leadership kind of name. Although it made the laughing stock and the butt of jokes throughout my school years, it has made me a better and stronger person.

So, the second daughter of the third daughter was on this planet named, but without a nickname. I figured that input was needed and would soon offer a suitable nickname. Now this is kinda how doing the nickname thing goes. You nickname a baby based on some characteristic, being physical or environmental or whatever. Now the first daughter of the third daughter was christened Lisa, a common Maya name, and nicknamed Negra, Spanish for black as she was quite dark at birth. This is not an uncommon calling and today in her teens, she is still called Negra by her family and friends. I know a young boy in another village that had a physical appearance at birth that prompted visitors to say, "Oh" when they first saw him. To this day, he is still "Oh" to the village. He has a cousin called Duvalin, after the sweet candy he craved as a youngster.

(It is probably a good time to digress into a lesson in Spanish grammar. I have taken great pains, well maybe not GREAT pains, but I have been careful to distinguish between naming and calling. There is a difference in Spanish. When you meet a speaker of Spanish you do not ask them their name, but rather, *¿Como se llama?* which is literally "what do you call yourself?")

The child in question here was named Zazil de Jesus. Zazil is Mayan (Maya is the people, an adjective etc., Mayan is the language, lots of people get that confused as in "that is a Mayan calendar"—WRONG!) for light, so the little girl is named Light of Jesus. We don't name children like that in my culture, thankfully, since I could easily have been "Diversion of Judas" or something similar. Well, Zazil being without a nickname was no problem, for me anyhow. Given the influences on her while she was in the womb, I freely offered and began to use "Tobita" in memory of the village's very own and memorable Uncle Toby. Everyone else soon began to call her Tobita, but always with a chuckle. I have this village life pretty much figured out!

Upon my next visit I learned that the family had re-nick-named Zazil . . . sit down before reading further . . . in keeping with the Maya village traditions . . . re-nicknamed Zazil, Valerie! Now exactly what part of this little Maya girl looked like a Valerie? Go figure! I saw that I obviously still had a lot to learn about Maya life, so I keep going back to Tinum.

11

The Road to Punta Allen

The road was worse this time than any other trip I have made to this remote spot that seems as though it could be at the end of the earth. Were it any worse, it would not have been passable.

A friend of many years accompanied me on this trip. Due to my totally undeserved reputation for exaggerating half of what I say and fabricating all the rest, my friend just laughed when I tell him that our destination is just a little over twenty six miles past Las Ranitas (our beer stop before commencing the journey) and that stretch of road will take us about three hours in my small VW Jetta. Another type of vehicle might make it a little safer for the vehicle, like not cutting your gas line as I did on my last trip, but it won't get you there any faster. Well, maybe a Humvee could.

Soon after Las Ranitas (Spanish for "little frogs" and owned by, you guessed it, a couple of French women), we entered the Sian Ka'an biosphere. The biosphere is a fifteen million acre preserve managed with ecological and environmental (am I redundant here?) friendliness and protects an incredible wealth of tropical plant and marine life, animals, birds, reptiles, and coral reefs. But maybe its most important role is that it puts a screeching halt to the massive, irresponsible, out-of-control resort development that runs for over sixty miles along what is now referred to as the "Maya Rivieria". Were it not for the Sian Ka'an, this development, with all its threats to the environment, would run all the way to Belize and probably eventually crumble from all the destruction it is doing. It may happen anyway.

The road around Las Ranitas is a combination of washboard, potholes (called *baches* "bah chays"), and washouts. It is sand, dirt, and hard sharp rocks. Basically it is an obstacle course. My friend just laughed when I said, "and that was the good part of the road." Upon entering Sian Ka'an, the vista was void of beach cabanas, dive and snorkel shops, and places for rubs, massages, and various other things usually found off the beaten path. One thing for certain, we were off the beaten path!

The road did, in fact, get worse. It was sometimes two car-widths wide, but more often only one car-width wide with occasional pull-offs to facilitate oncoming traffic. The washboard disappeared, but the washouts and the baches became larger and more numerous. We had now reached decision time. We had to decide which side of the road was less treacherous, decide to try to straddle a bache or not, if not, decide which side of the car should be gently driven into the bache, or decide that we needed to drive all four wheels into the bache.

Without pavement or dwellings of any kind, the tropical vegetation grew right up to the sides of the road, creating the effect of driving through a long serpentine tunnel of green. The road generally followed the shoreline. It is on a peninsula, so there was shoreline on both sides, but not visible through the thick tropical growth. My friend asked if we would ever see the shoreline and just about then, about ten miles into the journey, brilliant hues of blue appeared on both sides of us. On one side was Ascension Bay with deep blue waters and dark green leaves of the mangroves creating small islands of trees. On the other side, as far as one could see, were strips of deep blue to turquoise Caribbean waters rolling up on spits of near white sand beaches.

Boca Paila

This place is called Boca Paila (*boca* is mouth, I have no idea what *paila* is) and here the waters of the bay and sea meet under a few hundred feet of wood slats creating a bridge, albeit without guardrail of any kind. One should have a steady hand and keen eye here. Actually the bridge is much improved. The slats runs crossways now; they used to run the direction you were traveling. Slats used to be missing, and others were loose so that when your tire was on one end of the slat, the other end rose up into the air. On one trip over the bridge while under reconstruction, there were 10" or 12" wide slats laid out in a row, one row for each side of the car. I am appreciating the new bridge.

Boca Paila is the first time travelers want to stop the car to take photos. This is but just the first of many times people stop for photos during the next two-hour drive. This was not my first time at Boca Paila, but it was still awe-inspiring to break out from under the canopy of green into this beautiful scene. We made all the right stops for photos. We had been traveling for about an hour, right on schedule, but schedules are irrelevant here.

As we got back into the car I said, "and now for the bad road!" Again, my friend laughed in disbelief.

The baches got even wider and deeper. The jagged rocks were sticking up higher. The palm fronds were whipping the sides of the car as we tried, often in vain, to keep the car out of the baches. The road now was mostly one lane wide. Some baches now were the width of the road and we tried to pick the spot in the baches with the less jagged rocks. After five miles or so, it began to worsen, and I began to wonder if we were going to make it to the end of the peninsula. There had been a heavy rain the night before, and some baches held water. We now had small lakes to negotiate, sometimes twenty feet wide and thirty or more feet long. The water was murky so there was no way to know the depth of the bache or there more baches inside the bache or where the jagged rocks might be. Generally, we were able to negotiate the temporary lakes slowly and had few problems. I noticed that my traveling buddy had become a keen lookout for baches and rocks.

These baches were sand and rock, and often there were tire tracks to show us where other vehicles had, successfully we assumed, found their way through. Dirt and rock baches were another challenge. They generally were not as deep as the sand and rock baches, but the bache and strips of road before and after were covered with a slippery and slimy mud, often fifty to sixty feet or more. We could not go slowly without getting bogged down in the mire, and we were swerving and fishtailing back and forth attempting to avoid what rocks we could spot. Other vehicle tracks disappeared in the mud so we were on our own. Just shy of three hours from Las Ranitas, we arrived at the little Maya fishing village at the end of the road, my friend, my little VW Jetta, about fifty pounds of mud, and me.

This was Punta Allen and our destination was Sirena's. Sirena (Spanish for "mermaid" and this mermaid deserves her own story) lived all the way across the village that is about eight blocks long and three blocks wide, so we carefully drove the sand streets avoiding poultry, pork, canines, and a few old men that got into the hooch a little early that day. There is something about Sirena that must be a magnet for unusual people and events that the run-of-the-mill folk never encounter, making an average day with Sirena one of unexpectedness, excitement, urgency, sometimes bordering on chaos. Today was one of those days. Between all that was swirling around Sirena and her new friend that shipwrecked here three weeks before, I was wondering if we would ever break away and sink our toes into the sand. Finally I rose up and said, "My friend here just came from sixteen inches of snow, and I have to put his butt on the beach!" Our accommodations consisted of the first floor of a two-story beach house with a thatch roof. We had two bedrooms, five beds in all, and full-sized bath, kitchen, living, and dining rooms. In the back, facing the varied blues of the Caribbean, a sand floor porch ran the width of the house. The experience of the road called for a drink or two, or three. I vaguely remember Sirena, my friend Claudio, and me at Cuzan's that evening with some shrimp, lobster, and fish.

What I do remember of the night are the sounds of the gentle waves rolling up upon the shore a few feet away and the palm

Our humble abode

fronds rubbing together in the tropical breeze. The sounds took my mind off of the thumping bass rhythm of the band playing four blocks away in the town square. We never heard any melodies, just the constant beat of the bass. This was a special evening, so the local authorities kept the village electricity on for an extra two hours. Folks say it went until three o'clock in the morning, but I was only hearing the waters and the palms.

Daylight. The sea was tranquil. The colors from the rising of the sun on the water's edge extended for as far as I could see. There were no voices, no dogs barking, no roosters crowing, only the sounds of the sea and breeze. The sounds were occasionally interrupted by the hum of a fisherman's boat motor as he ventured out to earn his livelihood. Clocks and watches are of little value here, as in days of yore. (I need to do some research to find out just when yore was.) Time and lives here revolve around sunrises and sunsets. The days begin about six a.m. when the sun crawls up over the horizon on the Caribbean side of the peninsula and end about eight p.m. when the last light sinks into Ascension Bay. Then it's time to toast the day and on to bed.

It had been a busy day with much to do. We had to catch

the warmth of the sun on our faces, feel the salt breeze from head to toe, read a favorite book, test the warmth of the sea with our toes, take long solitary walks, allow the beautiful scene to soak in all the way to our bones, and check out the old lighthouse two kilometers or so further down the peninsula on a path through the palms and mangroves. Today was also the last of four days of *novenas* in celebration of the Virgin of Guadalupe. Throughout the country, the Virgin of Guadalupe is honored by groups carrying torches and running or biking a considerable distances. Each group had its own colors, matching sweat suits or commemorative T-shirts. The runners and bikers are followed by a truck or a bus that carries beverages, food, bicycle parts, and relief runners. Here in Punta Allen to commence the final day of honoring the virgin, they decorated a few fishing boats, loaded up some boom boxes, and filled the boats with children. They boated up and down the coast playing music and singing. It all culminated toward the end of the day at the small chapel in town with the pig dance. Normally my instincts would be to make light of

Decorated for the Virgin of Guadalupe

the concept of a pig dance, but I am married to someone who has done the chicken dance at various weddings. A pig dance can't be all that bad!

To do the pig dance requires preparation, unlike the chicken dance that can commence whenever the music strikes up. Also unlike the chicken dance, the pig dance requires first, foremost, and upfront, an animal, in this case, a pig. A participant in the culminating event then bakes or roasts or does whatever they want to do to the pig until it can't get any deader and is

Pig Dance

edible. The participant then procures an old fashioned metal tray with Coca Cola emblems all over it or some other type of tray or shallow basket. The tray or basket is then decorated with flowers and paper and cloth of red, white, and green. The head of the pig is placed on the tray or shallow basket and is also decorated, an apple in the mouth here and an occasional pineapple slice there. Some of the soon dancers-to-be saw fit to add further honor to the Virgin of Guadalupe by adding a couple of bottles of intoxicating beverages to the tray or shallow basket with the now decorated head of the pig.

The dancers at the chapel numbered eight or ten, and the other celebrants may have numbered forty of fifty. A boom box began to play, and the dancers began to shuffle their feet at various rhythms and steps, as indistinguishable a rhythm as the music had. The trays, pig head, beverages, and all were placed on their heads, and they circled around inside of the church for a while. After a few minutes of circling, the rhythm master led them out into the churchyard in conga line fashion and then led them into another circle pattern. The rhythm master's instrument was an old Coca Cola can with several used pop tops and maybe a few coins tossed in. Her rhythm was even less obvious that the dancers or the boom box's. Whenever a dancer seemed to tire, someone from the churchyard would jump in to relieve him or her. I am sure that what seemed like a couple of hours of dancing was really over in about fifteen minutes. At that point, the parts of the pig not used in the dancing were just a few knife strokes away from being part of free pork tacos and beer for everyone, with a

Pancho

greased pole climb to follow.

We decided that we had experienced just about all the excitement that we could handle in one day and retreated back to our isolated beach house with only the sounds of the sea and palms. It was a good day. I saw old friends and made new ones. One old friend was Pancho. Pancho is a handsome, big, friendly, passive golden lab. He has a habit of befriending visitors to Punta Allen and as in past visits, he could usually be found curled up at my feet while I read or wrote and only a step or two ahead of me on walks. As the light of day slipped into the bay, we toasted the day and fell asleep.

With the exception of the pig dance and decorated fishing boats, tomorrow promised to be pretty much like today, as would the next day, and the next. It doesn't take long for stress to melt away, worries to become forgotten, and for a peaceful spiritual oneness to come over you. For some it is a memorable experience; for others it changes a part of their lives. For all, it makes traveling down the road to Punta Allen a price worth paying.

December 2003

12

Wheat, Corn, and Birdseed

The Yucatán peninsula has, for me, three distinctive aspects. One is the beautiful Spanish colonial city of Merida where I work and live. The second is the presence of indigenous Maya villages where I visit and have dear friendships, and the third is the Caribbean coast where I totally relax and clear my mind.

All of my American friends need to fly or take a cruise ship to get to the Caribbean, but I can drive there! It generally takes me about four hours depending upon which route I take. When I go the Caribbean, I usually stay at a place named La Posada del Captain Lafitte. I have been staying there for about fifteen years and often brought new clients. The result is that in appreciation for my loyalty and bringing new business, I haven't paid the posted rates in years. I appreciate the discount! I am not the only repeat client. Most of their business is repeat business; so much so that there is a sense of being part of the Captain Lafitte family. What also happens is that year after year you often see the same people there and you can, and we have, developed good friendships. I am leaving in four days to go to Captain Lafitte to see friends from New York, Oklahoma, and Mississippi. We have a set of summer Lafitte friends and a set of Christmas-time friends.

OK, it is time to digress; I seem to do that a lot. In the early to mid 80s, I was trying to pull down a decent salary without working too hard as the Vice President for Business Stuff at a small college in eastern Pennsylvania. Colleges and universities, for your enlightenment, only compete on athletic fields and courts, and occasionally for a top notch faculty member. Other

than that, colleges and universities tend to be a tight and sharing community. It is a very sharing and caring industry, and we
all pretty much know each other across the country. The recent
tragedy that took place that took place at Virginia Tech was felt
by everyone in higher education because we all know that, but for
the grace of God, it could have happened to us.

The relevance of this is that while I was in eastern Pennsylvania, down the road a piece in the nation's capital, Gallaudet
University, a university for deaf students, was searching for a new
president. We always watch this things because possibly the new
president may have been a colleague at a previous institution,
you never know. Their board selected a woman from the University of North Carolina-Greensboro to be the new president. She
was not deaf, and the students staged an uprising and physically
closed down the university. This kind of display of student power
catches your eye if you are a vice president of a college. The
student's position was that the pool of candidates for the presi-
dency contained a deaf Gallaudet graduate who had taught and
administered at Gallaudet for some years and was qualified to be
the next president, and that they deserved to have a leader who
knew and understood the deaf culture. They had never had a deaf
president. The board capitulated and withdrew the offer to the
woman from North Carolina and selected the deaf man to be the
new president. I didn't know why, but I followed that story with
keen interest.

Several years ago during one of my visits to Captain Lafitte,
I was stationed at my usual position, the west side of the poolside cantina where I could look out over the pool at the turquoise
waters of the Caribbean and watch the cruise ships sail in and out
of the port on Cozumel island. I was wearing some clothing that
had "Elon" on it, and one of the two women sitting a few stools
away asked me if I was from Elon University. I explained that I
was Elon football's biggest and most avid fan, and that my sweet
wife was chair of the foreign language department at Elon. She
told me that she and her husband had a dear friend on the faculty
at Elon, and that he and his wife were god-parents of one of their
children. I asked for names and she replied, "Jim and Nancy

Pickens." Well, Jim and Nancy were good friends of ours, what a coincidence! Jim Pickens and the woman's husband had gone to graduate school together at the University of Tennessee. She also said that their husbands were out scuba diving and would return shortly and she knew they would like to meet us. Soon two men came up to the cantina, kissed the women on their cheeks and began talking with their hands. I don't mean waving hands about when we talk excitedly, but in sign language. They introduced themselves, and the husband of the woman who spoke to us was the president of Gallaudet University that I had read about twenty some years earlier. (The president of Gallaudet had an unusual name, "King Jordan.") The other man and his wife were on the faculty at Gallaudet, but not deaf. We saw them every year around Christmas time at Lafitte and became friends. What impressed me most about the four from Gallaudet was that they were the most joyous people I have ever been around.

Back in North Carolina, we kept up our friendship with Jim and Nancy over the years. We have hosted them in our homes in North Carolina and Yucatán, and we have visited their home on numerous occasions. The year 2007 was a momentous year for both King and Jim, well, probably for their wives too. King announced his retirement from Gallaudet after many years of distinguished service to the school. A new president was selected. Spurred by some dissident faculty, the students staged a repeat of the 1980s, closed the campus, and made what should have been a joyous farewell into a very unpleasant and disappointing year. Jim experienced a very different occurrence. At the age of fifty-five, he was diagnosed with a condition similar to Alzheimer's and needed to take a medical leave from Elon and then eventually take an early retirement with a medical disability. It was a crushing end to a distinguished and respected career spent teaching not only psychology, but also peace and caring for the less advantaged of the world. As an example, Jim often led student groups to Guatemala on Habitat for Humanity missions.

I think that just about every year we would suggest to Jim and Nancy that they should join us at Lafitte over the holidays and see their old friends King and Linda. They always declined citing family obligations, their own children and grandchild to consider. In 2007 they decided that they should do some special things while Jim was still able to participate and enjoy them, and they accepted our invitation to come to Merida and then to Capitan Lafitte over Christmas and New Years. A third couple, mutual friends, would join us also. We spent about a week enjoying Merida and then went to the Caribbean and La Posada del Capitan Lafitte to see King and Linda and enjoy the beauty of the place. Nancy had mentioned to me that she thought the Jim and King needed some defining moment to begin their retirements, a ceremony of some kind. So, just before we left Merida, I stopped in a supermarket and bought a supply of wheat seeds, corn kernels, and birdseed.

We arrived safely at Lafitte and spent a few days seeing old friends, enjoying the warm beautiful waters of the Caribbean and the wonderful food. One day just before sunset, we borrowed some torches from the staff and put the torches on either side of two plastic chairs near the water's edge. We invited Jim and King, wives, King's children, and friends to join us at the torches as Jim and King sat in the chairs. I asked King's children to assist me. I asked his daughter to translate my words into sign language for King and his son to help me with the seeds. Now, this next part may not be totally accurate but it was meant to be symbolic. I took the bag of wheat seeds and sprinkled the in a circle around Jim and King explaining that the seeds in Maya represented work and for their adult lives they have lived within a circle and the confines and restraints of work. Even when they would go as far away from their work as Yucatán, they still needed to return to their work. I asked them to notice that some of the seeds were blown away in the wind, others washed away by the waters, and yet others eaten by birds, and I kept replenishing the circle of wheat seeds. I explained this represented all the changes in their work over the years: changing jobs, changes in colleagues, and changes in technology.

I asked the son to anoint them with the corn. I explained that the corn was a Maya symbol of family, and anointing them represented the loving wives and good children that believed in them and supported them over the years. Last was the birdseed. My sweet wife sprinkled the birdseed over Jim and King. I said that the different seeds that comprised the birdseed represented friends, and that throughout their lives there were different kinds of friends that brought different kinds of gifts and blessings in their lives. I invited the wives to come and stand behind them.

I asked the four of them to look for the wheat seeds and notice that the sea and wind and birds had pretty much taken all the seeds away. This meant that their work, with all the confines and restraints, as well as the rewards, were gone and that they now needed to live their lives with a new orientation, an orientation of their choosing. I asked them to rise and, armed with the riches of family and friends, take their loving wives and began their new journey with a walk down the beach.

I glanced down the beach and saw two couples embraced in a kiss. Like the good guy cowboys of old, I reckoned that my work was done here and that it was time to take the torches and mosey on down to the poolside saloon and have me a double rum on the rocks.

13

Are-Ray-See-Faye

Gimmie an Are
     Gimmie a Ray
         Gimmie a See
            Gimmie a Faye
               What does that spell?

Arrecife, well kinda spells arrecife. That is where my friend Claudio and I are, at Arrecife Yucatán. Arrecife is Spanish for reef and we are technically staying at Reef Yucatán except that there is no reef here. There is a reef about eight hours by boat out in the Gulf of Mexico, but not here. Reef Yucatán is an all-inclusive resort.

Claudio and I met (not originally) at a watering hole in the Bush International Airport and flew down to Yucatán together. I sat next to a guy from Des Moines, Iowa, who was exciting as corn growing, but that's a whole other absence of a good story. Upon arrival, Claudio and I spent two days exhausting ourselves with activities in Merida.

On the first day we went to the super *mercado* to stock up. No one had been in the house, which meant an empty refrigerator, for five months. We encountered no problems finding the required tortillas, rum, and wine. That pretty much shot the day, and we had very little strength left to do anything except maybe some fine dining. The second day we took my computer, which was having a near death experience, into the shop where the young receptionist refused to believe that I was Vicente Fox,

President of Mexico, and she should send the bill to the federal government. I thought that I was doing very well using made-up technical terms to describe my particular problem until she disappeared and came back with a speaker of English, sort of. I toned down my techno speak as I was doing this in his second language,, and I didn't want to overwhelm him. The Spanish thing, or lack of, probably stems from my native Mexican accent due to having learned much of my Spanish amongst the indigenous Maya. Exercising our Spanglishes, we determined that this was going to be a cash, not credit card, deal. That shot pretty much ten or fifteen minutes of that day. Maybe we could squeeze in some more fine dining.

Day three we figured that we had enough strength to mash down the pedals of the VW Jetta and headed out of town. We stopped for lunch at a fishing village on the gulf coast and had fresh seafood at an open-air restaurant at the foot of a four mile long pier and felt the gentle warm salt air rolling over us. On the way down the coast we stopped at a flamingo (the big pink bird, not the Spanish dancers) reserve to see how close to land they might be on that particular day. They weren't, but often we could spy rows of pink out in the *cienaga*. (Yes, that *cienaga* where the Maya used to mine the salt out of the gulf waters and use it for trade throughout the Maya world.) After running out of any visible population along the coast we came upon our destination, Reef Yucatán, and checked in.

Reef Yucatán is rather large and was accommodating a couple of groups and a handful of couples and families. I generally expect to see people at an all-inclusive resort that look like, well, you know—svelte, charming, intelligent, can afford to be there—people like me! The larger of the two groups there struck me at first as a convention of Mexican cleaning ladies, very plain, unadorned, rather indigenous looking. None of them wore resort type clothes likes shorts and sandals and straw hats and T-shirts of other places we have been. These women were all dressed in their Sunday Go To Meetin's. Claudio suspected that they were not cleaning ladies, but actually were church ladies attending a convention and studying up on the Good Book and stuff like that.

My room faced the sea with a nice balcony. The breeze was wonderful. Problem was that it was on the third floor. I am three days away from taking a wheelchair through the Houston Bush the 1st International Airport and here I am dragging more things than I needed to bring up three flights of stairs. It will take some numbing with Bacardi if I am running up and down these stairs all day. The floors, the walls, the balcony,, and the drapery were all various shades of coral. This was broken up by bedspreads about the same color as the palm fronds waving outside the balcony. The palm fronds blocked some view of the sea, but on the other hand, they also blocked direct flights of seagulls, frigates, and egrets into the room.

I was pleased to see more beach than I had remembered. Hurricanes and strong storms from the north constantly reshape the beaches. Two years ago, Hurricane Isadore reshaped Reef Yucatán to mounds of rubble. Isadore made landfall right here, Reef Yucatán, in Telchac Pueblo. I came through here soon after. The great 100-foot-tall thatch roofs that gave Reef Yucatán its unique appearance were strewn all about. There was rubble everywhere. The fishing fleet of Telchac Pueblo next door was pretty much destroyed. There wasn't a street lamp, a telephone pole, an electric pole, or a medium-sized tree standing as far as you could see. The rains inland produced so much water that the village was cut into pieces by new rivers made by the water working its way to the sea. Today, there are still piles of wrecked fishing boats, beyond repair and abandoned. The reconstruction has gone nicely at Reef Yucatán and in the village Telchac Pueblo. Take heart, New Orleans.

Ah, ol' Claudio was right, the ladies were a fundamental evangelical church group, Church of the I'm-Never-Gonna-Wear-Make-Up-and-Frown-Real-Hard-on-Those-That-Do. The good thing about a group like this is that they don't take up much space at the bar. The other group was a bunch of turtle huggers.

Morning came way too early for me, but it was here and I had to deal with it. Unless a storm is approaching, mornings on this part of the gulf are very calm. The breeze is calmer, the water calmer, the palm fronds wave instead of dance in the breeze, and the gulf water is bluer. I could use a cup of coffee, but the restaurant is overrun by ladies in their Sunday Go To Meetin's from the Church of I've-Never Had-Any-Fun-and-I-Am-Sure-Not-Gonna-Start-Now. Not only that, I feel underdressed next to them. Can't wait for a prayer meeting to start!

The turtle huggers are checking out today. CONEFI is the acronym for the group; I didn't find out what it meant, just that was about turtles. Having turtles drawn on the back of the T-shirts that they all wore was a giveaway. I too am a turtle hugger in my own right. Ask me someday about my very own up front and personal first time turtle experience, and I will regale you with my story. I won't tell it now other that to say that it involved me, a 300-pound mother loggerhead, over a hundred billiard-ball-sized eggs, and over a hundred 1½-inch baby loggerheads trying to find the sea.

The upside of the moment is that the women of the Church of Where-it's-At-Now are off praying somewhere and it is very quiet. Time now to listen to the birds in the coconut palms, the waves gently washing ashore, and the gentle sounds of palm fronds. Someone just started a lawnmower.

The funeral for Lorenzo the lawn mower guy will be next Thursday.

Children, natural-born yard apes, are constant liars. "Hey! Did you remove you sister's eye with Uncle Larry's Rotor Rooter equipment?" "No, but she hit me first!" Like just now, they are in the pool happily playing, no, ratchet that up a notch to frolicking, in the pool. Their little bodies are saying, "This is sooooo much fun, come on in." I did and found the water fit for a polar bear . . . those lying little kids.

The funerals for all the little children in the pool will be next Friday.

The women of the Church of This-Is-The-Only-Group-That-Will-Take-Me are still off somewhere. Can't be prayers, they haven't sinned enough to pray this long. Must be extra sessions on being plain and unadorned.

For the uninformed, all Mexican music is alike except Armando Manzanero, whom I don't take seriously because his name, to me, means "apple picker" and he is an *alux* (Maya version of a leprechaun) and he writes and sings love songs for full-sized women, which in Yucatán could be as much a 4'11". The rest of Mexican music is lyric- and melody-less and consists of just a pounding rhythm that can be played non-stop for days. Such a piece of music is playing on the pool speakers right now.

The funeral for the pool speakers is scheduled for right after their demise which Claudio and I have planned for about 3:00 am tonight.

I don't know how much coastline there is in Mexico, but I know that there is a lot. The Pacific lines both the west and south. The east is the Gulf of Mexico and the Caribbean. It has to be a few thousand miles of coastline and in a word, it's blue. The sky over Yucatán is the bluest sky I have ever seen. Eighteen miles out to sea it blends with the varying blues of the water. (A five foot eight inch person can see eighteen miles before the curvature of the earth takes the vista away. Look it up!) Blue is warm, blue is calming, blue beckons you. What I find so curious is that here in the midst of the ancient and contemporary Maya, they have no word for blue. They have words for red, black, green, yellow, but no word for blue. I have a dictionary with a Maya word for blue, but I have checked it out with my Maya friends, and the dictionary is wrong.

There is a massage table complete with therapist at one end of the pool. Is it just me or isn't a good massage something that shouldn't be done in public, especially in front of little children lying about water temperatures? The women of the Church of I-Plan-To-Never-Sin-Again are lining up at the massage table about as much as they are lining up at the bar. The catch phrase on the massage pamphlet was "offering complete relaxation." This is not included with the food and beverage. I was completely relaxed last night with Bacardi, it was cheaper, and I didn't have to moan and groan in front of lying little yard apes! Nonetheless, I take the pamphlet and read on.

The first choice is named *piedras calientes*. My Spanish is sufficient to know that means "hot stones". The thought of hot stones and my skin together is not totally relaxing. Next one is an energetic Maya massage. Now at the risk of insulting a culture, this is a little oxymoronic for me. Please hear me out. I consider the Maya to be about the hardest working people I have even seen. However, due to the often horrendous heat and humidity here, they have learned to pace themselves at about half the speed of smell. That and energetic don't go together for me. They tried to fool me with the next one. The Zazil Ha massage. They just happened to hit on two of the ten Maya words I know. *Ha* is Maya for water. If a Maya does a double *ha*, or *ha ha*, he is not saying water water. Make a quick check to see if your fly is open. I have a little friend (who does not lie!) named Zazil de Jesus, which means light of Jesus. So they have a light water massage, I had a chemistry course; all water weighs the same. OK, in Spanish it is common to put the adjective after the noun so then we would have water light. Water also has no calories, how could it be water light? I think that they are just messing with the tourists with that one. We finish the list with a seaweed wrap. I am claustrophobic and have smelled seaweed. 'Nuff said!

I am watching a steady stream of women of the Church-Of-Jesus-Loves-Me-But-He-Can't-Stand-You heading for the exit. They still look 100% indigenous to me, as though they came from a hundred different jungle villages, unable to afford a place like this, looking out of place, and yet, almost to a person, they were all pulling an airport rolling carry-on bag just like they were going to an airport. I have some relaxing that needs to be done!

Another quiet morning. The blues of the sea and sky are layered as far and as high as you can see. High above, frigates are gliding effortlessly in the air currents. If there is any flap to the wing, it is indiscernible to the naked eye. They take left turns, right turns, and each turn gets wider and farther away until the winds make them double back.

No new groups have checked in to replace the turtle huggers and the women from the Church of I-Love-Jesus-So-Much-I-Can't-Stand-It. The folks that are left respect the quiet. They walk and you don't hear footsteps. In place of the demonstrative hugs so common here, there are just little nods of recognition and maybe a "*buen dia*," a softer quieter version of *buenos dias*, "good morning." Couples of all ages are holding hands, and mothers have small children in their arms or at their sides still too sleepy to exercise the giggles and shrieks of joy that will come later in the day.

Claudio and I did not get up at 3:00 am to demolish the pool speakers, so that we know that soon the activities director will interrupt the calm with announcements of volleyball and ping pong tournaments and that the sea is calm enough for kayaks. We accomplished our mission here of doing absolutely nothing and we think it best to quietly slip away. So we did.

14

On a Mission From God

The great crusades were attributed to being a mission from God. The movie *Blues Brothers* revolved around a mission from God. Those events were far from the missions and missionaries that I knew of as a child growing up in a mission-oriented Protestant congregation.

Missionaries, as I recall, felt "called" to go to a Bible College or near equivalent, and then "called" again to forsake the comforts of pastoring a suburban or rural congregation and all the middle class living that goes with it to go into a mission field.

They had to develop a "dog and pony" show, and I mean that in a nice way, to present information and encouragement to congregations sufficient to secure enough financial support to uproot their families and trek off to deep dark Africa or India or China or somewhere where they were two thousand miles from aspirin and combated leprosy and leopards on a daily basis.

Each year they returned to the dog and pony circuit and explain that they almost have converts and that the congregation should fund their way back to deep dark wherever. In all fairness to missionaries, they do learn to be humble.

So here I am in Yucatán in my little city of nearly a million people with five-star restaurants and every amenity you could want from a city. I am buying plants for a dollar apiece to adorn my newly redecorated patio. A vehicle drives up and a pleasant, well-dressed woman exits the vehicle. The vehicle is a $40,000 SUV with Texas plates. I have seen such vehicles at the American Consulate, which is a hotbed, so I am told, for DEA activity. I always speak to other obvious Americans that I meet, but the DEA always seem reluctant to talk. So I provokingly ask the oft asked questions, "So what brings you here all the way from Texas and what part of town are you living in?"

"We live in the neighborhood Hacienda San Antonio, (I know it well, an upper middle class neighborhood), and we have been missionaries here for ten years," was the reply. I wanted to say, "Ya mean, ya mean," (my voice goes up an octave on the second ya mean), that I am paying my own way, albeit rather inexpensive, to live in this sometimes paradise and many of my friends wish they could do the same, and you've got churches paying for you to live in an upper middle class neighborhood, visit museums, theaters, five star restaurants, tropical beaches, symphonies, and drive a $40,000 SUV!" But I don't say anything; I just smile and wish her a nice day.

Wow! They get people generally earning a little above the poverty line in the U.S.A. to send them here and suffer the temptations of materialism and bounty!

My evening prayer this summer day in Yucatán . . .

Dear God (I hope she is listening),

Thank you for showing me today that my life here may be some kind of mission. By the way, do I get anything extra, like stars in my crown or something, for having paid my own way?

15

Handbook on Why & How to Obtain a Mexican FM3

To all future seekers of an FM3: There is no accurate information on just how to obtain an FM3. Trust me, I have just gone through the process, and I can relate to you first hand that all the information that you get, including the official looking stuff on the internet, is a bucket of hooey! This is dedicated to you in a spirit of public service; frankly I have better things to do than write a handbook.

Background

I have been coming to Yucatán since 1989, four or five American presidents ago; we may have had a good one in there. I don't know, I don't even remember them all. More than just coming to Yucatán since 1989, I actually lived here for the better part of five years, 1999 – 2004, and now in 2007 may have moved back again. The jury is still out. A lot will depend on how a new business enterprise goes. For all of those years, I never had anything but a 90 or 180 day tourist visa. I always returned to the states for the American football (as to distinguish between other countries definition of football) season, university level. Early on during this stint, I opened bank accounts, bought a home, bought a car, paid taxes, and have always done just fine on a tourist visa. I have had absolutely no need to spend money to obtain a more permanent status, an FM3 or eventually an FM2 residency.

Until now.

One Why

Mexican immigration only grants a stay for 90 or 180 days on a tourist visa. Neither God, nor the Virgin of Guadalupe, nor I, know why this is true, and they are certainly clueless at the immigration offices. They can never accommodate a need, like, "I've only got 179 days left on my passport, so just give me 170 days". No, it is 90 or 180. I guess that they have picked up a few dynamite policy tips from USA immigration, or government in general. You would figure that the culture that invented the concept of the zero could be more flexible mathematically. (How would you configure a computer without a zero?) For me, all this meant that since I have a client coming down to Yucatán in 150 days, that before my 120 is up and I still have 120 days on my passport, I would need to drive my truck 2,000 miles back to the border, cross into Texas, stay a day, return for another 120 days, and drive another 2,000 back to Yucatán. That is some serious time and expense for a math deficiency!

(Note: Ah my friend, why not just drive over to Belize for a day, isn't that a lot closer? I am not taking my brand new truck to a drug-infested country for an hour, let alone overnight.)

Obtaining an FM3 is a fraction of the cost of leaving and re-entering the country.

Another Why

I did not know that after I set up my banking here, bought the house and car, etc., that they changed the laws the following year and required an FM3 to do all this stuff. Not only can you not open a bank account without an FM3, you cannot even slightly tinker with one that has been grandfathered in, even though your new business enterprise may need to wire a few zillion pesos to the bank. An alternative, of course, is to buy a tent and set up camping by an ATM machine and withdraw the zillion or so pesos 3,000 at a time. It could make you late for an appointment.

How

How – Internet:

Surf the internet. There are several official looking internet sites that explain the process and documentation necessary for the office of immigration. I could give you the web site addresses but you will print out a ton of stuff, run out of ink and paper, find out that the information is conflicting and inaccurate ,and get mad at me. But, you NEED TO DO THIS STEP so that when your friends ask if you checked the internet, you can say, "yes."

How – Passport Check:

Check your passport for the expiration date. You need to have a little over thirteen months left on your passport to begin the FM3 residency process. If you do have over thirteen months before expiration, go directly to column B. If not, stay with me here in column A, and I will walk you through your passport renewal.

How – Passport Renewal Step 1:

Sleep in. Don't go down to the USA Consulate and get caught in the throngs of locals trying to get visas to the USA. Wait for that traffic to clear and go down to the consulate later only to find that they close at 12:30 p.m. every day

How – Passport Renewal Step 2:

Try to check and see when our government may be giving special deals, say, to strawberry pickers or something. That creates very long lines that you want to avoid (Don't jump on my case about the strawberry pickers reference. I spent my youth making my money by picking strawberries, apples, raspberries, plucking chickens, snapping beans, etc., so if I could do it, so can anyone else who comes to the States!) Failing obtaining that information, go on down about 11:30 a.m. You will feel so fortunate. You have a passport, you just want it renewed. The other Americans there have all had their passports, wallets, and credit cards stolen in Cancun. Some of them lost their underwear. Don't get too caught up in their sad stories; there is little that you can do. When it is your turn, they will give you a short several-page form to fill out and instruct you to go down to Wal-Mart to get passport photos taken, and that would be American passport size 5x5 centimeters in color, not the 4x4 centimeter black and white Mexican size. They stress this. You can fill out the short several-page form while you wait fifteen minutes for your photos to be ready.

How – Passport Renewal Step 3:

Return to the consulate about the same time the next day. Oh, I forgot to mention that they take your belt and cell phone when you go in. Now, I didn't miss my cell phone, but I had lost some weight and drawers weren't exactly form-fitting, if you know what I mean, so I could have used the belt. The security guys like to act meaner than skunks when you enter, but are jovial and friendly when you leave. I did this step during President Bush's visit to Yucatán, and the security gave me a lot of good-natured teasing. Once inside, when it is your turn, you give them the form and Wal-Mart photos and your credit cards, which they promptly hit for a whopping $67, and ask you to come back in two weeks. You are out of there in five minutes. When you retrieve your cell phone and belt, you suggest to security that if they really wanted to be good world neighbors that they should keep President Bush. That kind of sets them off!

How – Passport Renewal Step 4:

Return in exactly two weeks like they asked and give security your belt and cell phone In five minutes you will have your new passport good for the full ten years. I have to say that these people are good! They are efficient, reliable, and helpful. I say let them all cross the border, but not to mow lawns or clean houses, let them run our government offices! They would be a dramatic improvement!

Column B:

How – FM3 Step 1:

Go downtown to the immigration office to learn that it has moved to the suburbs. Have some lunch, get a little drunk, take a cab home and wait for tomorrow.

How – FM3 Step 2:

Find the new location—wait, I think that you need some pre-information here, especially after the consulate experience.

Remember what I said about the internet? Well the same

can be said for everyone you will deal with in this process. Oh, don't shy away from the process. They will all be friendly, gracious, well-meaning, helpful, and somewhat inaccurate. The other issue at play here is that this process requires at least a good hour of work to complete on their part, but in order to maintain a stress-free environment and a staff with happy hearts as top flight, crack government appointees, you will only participate in this process ten minutes at a time and only one time per week. Remember that whatever you are told, it will be partially accurate.

That being said;

How – FM3 Step 2 Revisited:

Find the new location in a beautiful old colonial home on the beautiful Avenida Colon in a beautiful neighborhood in beautiful Garcia Gineres at Calle 8. Stop at the card table on the porch and a really happy-hearted security fellow will invite you to sign in, and he will give you a numbered badge so that the staff will know in what order to serve you, more or less.

A word about the staff. The uniformed staff are all female, and this is how they feed their families. The male staff dress casually and appear to be of a different genetic makeup like maybe they have uncles in Congress or something. The uniformed female staff gets to handle all the paperwork, and the male staff gets to make thumping sounds when they stamp things and sign their names a lot.

You enter the beautiful old colonial home at the door that has a "push or pull" sign on it so that you won't bust your knuckles on the beautiful old wooden colonial door. There will be a uniformed female staff member at a reception desk who, with a happy heart, will explain to you in full detail the whole process. She will give you a printout of exactly what documentation you will need and exactly how much it will cost. You can return anytime, but it will probably take you a week to gather your documentation.

You leave the beautiful old colonial house, returning your numbered badge to the happy-hearted security guy who bids you a beautiful day.

OK – here is exactly what documentation you will need,

more or less:

1   A letter in Spanish to the director of this whole process, by name, obviously the person who God reports to since even God don't understand the whole process. Explain why you want residency, how long you have lived here, do you have a constant reliable income stream, and whether or not you want to work in Mexico. Never indicate a specific company because you lose your residency if you change jobs. I requested to be an independent teacher. Use flowery language; they like that a lot.

2   Two letters from locals recommending you for FM3 status stating that they have known you XX years, you are a really good, honest person, and that you don't smell bad. Be sure that your referees include address and telephone numbers.

3   Copy of your current tourist visa.

4   Copy of every page of your passport, even if it is new like mine and totally void of entries.

5   Proof of domicile. This could be your electric bill or water bill; I gave them a copy of everything so they could run out of file space quicker.

6   Proof of income. Provide at least three months of bank state-ment copies showing the income that you referenced in your letter. If you do internet banking, you can pull those state-ments off of the internet. I gave them bank statements show-ing the referred incomes, other bank statements showing some consulting income, and statements from all four of my Mexican accounts. I'm going for the record for the thickest file!

7   I topped it off with a copy of a note from my mother stating that even when I am sick, I still do my homework. It's a little dated but I figure that additional character reference won't hurt.

That pretty much shot the first week of the process.

How – FM3 Step 3:

Return to the big beautiful old colonial house, sign in, get your numbered badge, and enter. Proudly flash your documenta-tion to the uniformed female, and she will give you a little colored piece of paper with a number on it and point toward a door. Oh my God, there are uniformed female staff everywhere and no signage except to identify work stations as "A," "B," etc. You can stand there and look totally confused; it works, but can be a little more time consuming. Here's what you do. As you enter, turn left past the first two stations, and then turn right and go into the next room where there are three work stations. Sit down on one of the folding chairs, you will be called soon. When called, give the little numbered colored piece of paper to her, she must get paid per number or something, like how many bushels did you pick that day. If, and I say if, your documentation is acceptable and you don't have to repeat step 3, she will give you two poorly xeroxed copies of bills you will need to pay. However, they do not accept payment. They must have some kind of record for money management! Not to worry, you go down to the bank around the corner and pay them, and return in exactly one week with the paid bills and three copies of front and profile passport photos that cannot be from Wal-Mart instant cameras, but from a studio—4x4 black and whites, not the American 5x5 color.

How – FM3 Step 4:

Return in a week, same process, colonial house, badge, colored paper, happy hearts, etc. Only this time don't go in the back. Just go in, turn left, and sit down. It will seem as though no one notices you but eventually someone will call you up, take your colored piece of paper, and invite you to sit down again. You offer the photos but she doesn't want them. Eventually you are invited into the office of one of the young men who stamps stuff and signs his name a lot. He acts like he has thoroughly reviewed your files but his questions reveal otherwise. He asks you to choose your status, a pensioner or an independent teacher. He explains the rest of the process (I think that he is actually the one who approves your FM3) and invites you to return in exactly one week. In the meantime be sure not to lose those little passport photos!

How – FM3 Step 5:

Return in one week and you will notice that you are recognizing several other of the weekly visitors. This time go back to your original back room where no one seems to want to assist you. Eventually you are invited into a further back room where a young fellow will ask a lot of questions about things already covered and documented. He is verifying all the information and entering it into a computer. He also fingerprints you. Then he hits you with the stumper question: "How tall are you in meters?" More than one and less than two is about as close as I can get. He enters a guess. No weight question. Shucks, I know that one. He takes your photos, finally, and hand glues them to some sheets. He gives me a bill to pay, again at the bank. This one is nowhere close to the printed page at step one. It's not huge in dollars, but a sizable percentage off. He invites me to return in one week.

How – FM3 Step 6:

Can it be true? Can this really be the last step like the guy last week assured me? I did the routine, badge, colored paper, and asked which cotton-picking station I should go to now. Go in and turn left, right there. I was waited on, she took the paid bill copy and in a matter of minutes I had my FM3! I was appreciative and let her know that I would have kissed her every toe had she so wanted.

Footnote:

It was a ludicrous process, but everyone at every step was so darn nice that you just go with it and find things to appreciate. A month or more for an hours worth of real work is mind-boggling. Yet, now my mission is accomplished, and I feel a sense of pride to be an American-Mexican.

🦎 16 🦎

La Posada Rises

Everyone in the room raised their glass, glasses clinked for a few seconds, and then a loud, heartfelt "cheers" erupted. In a sense, a technical sense, I had some responsibility for the moment, but in my heart and head I took no responsibility at all.

The day started innocuously enough. I forgot to pay Lucy, remember Lucy, the faithful woman who cleans our house twice a week. "How in your Dutch cleanliness-is-next-to-godliness can you justify having your house cleaned twice a week?" (Hey! It's only once a week when we are gone!) We have tile and stone floors throughout the house and I go barefoot. After a couple of days of dust I am leaving footprints all over the place. I always lose at Hide 'n' Seek with the grandchildren. "Just follow the black footprints and you will find Tata, dear ones" ("Tata" being an indigenous term for grandfather). That, and when I am here alone the dishes seem to pile up in the sink rather quickly, so we have the house cleaned twice a week.

We were out of town about halfway to her village when I remembered that I forgot to pay her. Lucy? That's a pretty hip name for an indigenous cleaning woman. Well, Lucy is one pretty hip indigenous woman! Lucy has a cell phone! It was given to her and she is now learning how to use it. Now that's a doubly-hip indigenous woman!

TIME OUT for a computer word check...........

In the 30s and 40s, people were "hep." If you were a jazz musician you could be a "hep-cat." In the 50s and 60s, we were "hip." We could just be "hip," or "hip to" something. In the 70s and 80s, we went through being "cool" and "with it." I have no clue what the word or phrase is in this new millennium, so I keep using "hip". I also have a $25,000 artificial hip, so I am rather committed to the word.

So we turned the car around and headed back toward home. When we arrived, we paid Lucy and then tried to call our destination of the day to find out what roads were open or closed. We had tried from the car on our cell phone and weren't getting any answer. We didn't know if the problem was our American cell phone plan in a foreign country. No answer from the home phone either.

We left for the second time on the day's adventure. "How in your Dutch timeliness-is-next-to-godliness can you handle this delay?" We were going to be early but now we will be on time. "How can you write like this?" Probably dementia!

We turned right onto the *circuito* just outside our house. The *circuito* with several unmarked turns theoretically circles the old city, but now is in the middle of town. At the white rocket in the median strip the *circuito* makes an unmarked right turn, but we turned left out toward the *periférico*. The *periférico* also circles but outside of town. Once on the *periférico*, I knew that we had a left hand turn onto the road that runs across the peninsula at a traffic light soon after passing what may be the world's largest Coca Cola plant.

The *periférico* is four to six lanes wide; we are not sure which because there are no lines marking lanes. This invites a high speed free for all with cars trucks and motorcycles bobbing and weaving all over the road. It's great for anyone with a death wish. We passed the Coca Cola plant and I saw before us pavement rising up into the air. They had installed a bridge where the traffic light was. Do we exit before or after the bridge? Signage was nearly non-existent. I kept us in lane 3 ½ to keep our options open. Out of the corner of my eye I finally saw a sign and we bolted out from between two rather large trucks in our little VW Jetta and exited the *periférico* to the right running parallel to it. When we arrived under the bridge they had removed the signals and built a Boston-style traffic circle. This confirms the motto that came out of the Mexican revolution, "Just because things are working right, that doesn't mean we won't change them". We negotiated the traffic circle exiting east and headed out across the peninsula.

It was a good thing that we had bought a newspaper that morning. There was an article about one of the three options for crossing the peninsula being closed for another fifteen days to repair damage from Hurricane Wilma. We were concerned about the other two options. Although it was probably unnecessary, we stopped midway and refilled the gas tank, taking the opportunity to inquire about the roads. We wanted to know if we needed, for example, to head south into Guatemala, then east into Belize and then north back into Yucatán. They told us that our first choice was also closed and that the *cuota* road was the only option. "*Cuota*" means that we have the privilege of paying to drive on it.

The gas station would be our last contact with or glimpse of civilization until we reached the Caribbean coast. We had been traveling a couple of hours now, not counting the false start. After an hour on the *cuota* road we encountered our first visual reminder that Wilma had cut a swath through the jungle. The cuota road is normally a four lane paved divided highway (we don't pay to drive on dirt!). All of a sudden we were driving on dirt! Also, on both sides of the road was a lake that had never been there before. What makes that even more surprising is that Yucatán soil is so rocky and porous that the lakes and rivers are underground. This place was holding water! A little while later the road was down to two lanes as Wilma had torn out about three miles of the west bound lanes. The foliage had distinct black high water marks maybe two meters above the road. That would be our last sign of Wilma until we reached the coast. Our destination was where she had made landfall.

As we neared the back side of the Can Cun airport (yes, my friends, Can Cun is two words, shortened for the convenience for tourist brochures, etc. (*Can* in Maya is "snake;" I am not sure about *Cun*, but maybe something like "nest"). Can Cun is, in fact, about as charming as a nest of snakes!

OK, where was I? More signs of Wilma's visit began to

appear. Along the sides of the road we began to see piles and piles of *escombro* (rubble or debris) from destroyed homes, stores, and resort hotels that had been trucked out and dumped in the interior. When our road intersected with the coast road that runs down to Belize we saw more evidence. Probably 90 to 95 percent of the billboards advertising the resorts on the Maya Riviera were gone. In some respects, a positive cleansing effect of a hurricane!

Glancing eastward toward the coast, we saw several building that we had never seen before. No trees over ten to twelve feet tall were left standing, and the resorts that were once hidden amongst the palms were visible. Somewhere between thirty and forty-five minutes down the coastal road, we came upon a sign that indicated that we should turn off the main road onto a sand path that led to our destination, La Posada del Capitan Lafitte.

It was December 20th, on or about the winter solstice, when the days stop getting shorter and began to get longer again. I only know this because I was born June 20th, on or about the longest day of the year...at least it was for my mother.

About two months ago in October, toward the end of the hurricane season, the eye of hurricane Wilma tore across the island of Cozumel and made landfall right here in the Playa del Carmen area. We had received photos via the internet of the horrendous destruction in the area in general of La Posada del Capitan Lafitte specifically. The photos were crushing, heartbreaking.

Our lives in Merida, Yucatán started out several years ago as our special "getaway" from all things hectic and stressful. Later, as we began to host university student and faculty groups and as we keep up with repairs to the house, Merida, too, has become a place of too many things to do in too little time. La Posada del Capitan Lafitte had become our retreat, the one place where our lives were uninterrupted by telephones, television, internet, and other peoples problems. We could spend each day in sun, sand, and the blue Caribbean waters. Doing absolutely nothing at all was an art form. We would come over here at least twice a year for two or three days and have ourselves for ourselves. The rest of the year our lives seemed to belong to everyone else. Here at La Posada del Capitan Lafitte, we were cared for, pampered even, and honored. In October, we saw visual evidence that we may possibly never again have that special experience that is La Posada del Capitan Lafitte.

Only now as I write this, am I beginning to understand the importance of this December 20th. Only now as I struggle to find words do I begin, at the simplest level, to comprehend my own feelings and emotions.

Yes, there are other resorts on the Maya Riviera and there are other beaches in Mexico, in the world for that matter. But this place, La Posada del Capitan Lafitte is where Luis, Jose Luis, Manuel, Pedro, Julio, Victor, Jesus, Martin, Rafael, and the list goes on, practice their art of making you feel special. This is where the Dodgens from Seguin, Texas, come, as does the Graddy family from Tulsa, Oklahoma, the four friends from Gallaudet University, Laura and her folks from Baltimore, oh and we can never forget Lucas, the big black lab from Mississippi who has been coming down here since before the roads had pavement, with his owners Burl and Susanna. This is not a place; it is people. It is staff and patrons blending into a large family. Friendships are made here. We always look forward to seeing those friends the next visit. I could not bear the thought of not being in this place with those people again.

Still in October, again via the internet, we received a list of places that would reopen and when. La Posada del Capitan Lafitte was scheduled to reopen in November 2006. There was so much work to do, and it had to be more hurricane-proof next time. I could handle a year's absence. What was not known to me at the time was that the staff, facing a gift-less Christmas, mouths to feed, clothing to buy, electric bills to pay, and a strong sense that they were vested, not employed, in this place, brought forth an incredible spirit that said that there was enough still standing to reopen on a limited basis in two months. It would require a miraculous effort and unmatched determination, but it could be done with what they had left to work with, and replacing the totally destroyed and missing buildings could be spread out over the following year.

The work began and as the vision of reopening in two

months became more of reality, they began to contact people who had made reservations to see if they still wanted to come down. We heard about this via the internet and e-mailed to see if there was any way they might have room for us. They did.

So on the afternoon of December 20, 2005, we turned onto the two kilometer long sand path, which frankly was in better shape than before the hurricane. About half way down we began to see the entry arch. The closer we got, the more we realized that we did not see any buildings on the other side of the arch, only sand and thinly white capped waves. There were no buildings visible through the arch! As we approached the arch entry, the generally somber guards greeted us with wide smiles and waved us through. Oh my! There were wide stretches of beach where familiar buildings once stood! All but one of the entire front row of single and duplex cabanas were gone! The second row two-story cabanas were now "beach front with a view!" The towering palms were gone. Only short stubs of palms survived, many leaning at forty five degree angles, roots barely in the sand, and only a frond or two sticking out on top. The game room with its towering thatch roof was gone, leaving a ten-foot-wide sidewalk ending in the sand for no apparent reason. The "take one/leave one" library/TV/restroom building was gone! The lower level of the restaurant was gone!

We drove up to the circle to unload our bags and the staff, Luis, Jose Luis and the others, came pouring out from the recep-

tion area to greet us. Officially they had reopened on December 15th, but today was the first day that anyone came down the sand path for a stay. Today was the first day that any part of the La Posada del Capitan Lafitte family came back to honor and share in all the incredible work that had been done. There our friends stood to greet us. We got out and exchanged kisses and hugs and joked about all the units having "beach front with a view" and how beautiful so much beach was. I realized at that moment that these buildings, past and present, meant nothing to me. All that mattered was that these wonderful people were alive. We hugged them all again. I never again noticed the missing buildings or the bedraggled palms; seeing our special friends made the place beautiful again.

We settled into and left our room quickly to take our anointed places, the stools on the west side of the poolside bar where we could watch the layered hues of blue in the pool, sea, and sky. Yes, the pool and the bar survived. More hugs and kisses were exchanged with Jesus and Victor. They asked if we wanted "the usual." We nodded, they brought us our drinks, and La Posada del Capitan Lafitte was officially back!

We were there only a few minutes when I spied specially-abled Laura from Baltimore and her parents Jim and Bardell coming up the steps. Oh how wonderful, the family is gathering! We raced over for yet more hugs and kisses.

In all, there were four parties totaling sixteen people this special December 20th at La Posada del Capitan Lafitte. Three parties of us returnees were joined by one family of newcomers. We quickly brought them—Stephanie, Gordon, Sarah, and Will (older brother Ben arrived the next day)—into the group. We all gathered for dinner about the same time, getting caught up or getting to know each other. The sixteen of us got closer as our worlds got smaller.

I have never been the perfect or best son, ball player, father, employee, employer, or spouse, but I knew at this moment, I was in the right place at the right time, and I was where I should be on this December 20th in history. Now, this is where I technically became responsible for the toast mentioned at the beginning. I told Manuel (did I tell you there were more hugs and kisses with the wait staff?) that I wanted to buy a drink for everyone. My Dutch frugalness-is-next-to-godliness had calculated that my maximum

The Jolly Rogers were everywhere – in old tree stumps, on trees, on cannons, everywhere -- showing the pride and determination of the staff.

exposure was sixteen drinks, and one of them was for a child. We got over the linguistic/language issue of translating one big drink with sixteen straws to one more of what everyone else was already drinking. I turned to my beloved and asked, "Honey, can you do this for me? I will emotionally fall apart if I try it."

She garnered everyone's attention and said, "Please raise your glasses high and honor the reopening of La Posada del Capitan Lafitte and the incredible efforts of the men who made this happen." Glasses clinked, "Cheers" erupted, and like the mythical phoenix rising up out of its own ashes, La Posada del Capitan Lafitte had risen up out of its own rubble.

P.S. How could there possibly be a P.S. to all this? Early in the next afternoon a taxi pulled up and out came King, Linda, Joe, and Carol from Gallaudet University! More family was gathering! In December 2005, my hometown Chicago White Sox had won the World Series, my favorite Big Ten team, Penn State, had won the conference in football, Joe Paterno had been named coach of the year, and the La Posada del Capitan Lafitte family was back together again. I could die a very happy man right now!

With special thanks to Michael Graddy, Luis Rivera, and Jesus Lizama

17

Sotuto

It was a Sunday night as we drove under the big sign saying "Bienvenudo a Sotuto." We found our way to a small chapel not far from the village square. The father of the groom struggled a little in his second language, Spanish, asking us to move our cars from the end of the block and put them in front of the chapel so that they would be in all the photos. They are some cars in the village, generally quite old, but we are the only guests to arrive at the wedding in cars. Most walked if local. Those who came from a distance came packed standing up in the back of flatbed trucks.

Several men and women came over to greet us in Maya or in Spanish. I assumed that it was in order to have a memory of actually meeting tall sophisticated city people or fair-haired *gringos*. I later came to understand that they were family members of the bride and groom thanking us for coming to the blessed event.

The small chapel was full. There is seating for maybe one hundred and twenty. As honored guests, we were directed to the white plastic chairs instead of the old rickety wooden folding chairs. I, for one, would have chosen to stand rather than to trust the welfare of my tailbone to one of those old chairs that has earned the antique flaky paint look with years rather than artistry. The chapel is quite plain. Strings of flower petals are stung in parallel with the roofline. The walls are bare. There is no crucifix here or altar. There are no robes on the clergy. This will be a Protestant wedding in the heart of five hundred years of Catholic mission and influence.

Everyone is dressed to the hilt. The older women wear classic white *huipils* with the brightly colored embroidery, the younger women their finest dresses that we would place, fashion wise, in the 1920s or '30s. The men too displayed generational differences with the older men wearing *guayaberra* dress shirts and the younger "modernized" ones in shirts and ties, some even in suits and ties. When the ceremony started, it was apparent that the suits and ties were clergy.

There were faces, one hundred and twenty wonderful faces on these beautiful folk, not counting the ones who came by car. Many had the classic Maya face, profile, and features...weathered faces but soft and gentle, reflecting their demeanor. So many of the young girls had a stunning beauty about them. The precious little ones always have special faces in Sotuto or in any other small village in this ancient region. They ignite a passion to hug them, scoop them all up, and take them home with you. Their eyes dance in wonderment at this special event. They have lightning quick smiles and sometimes a shy giggle as they look at one of the visiting *gringos* who looks like he just might be Santa Claus in street clothes right here in their little village.

Imagine if you can, Santa Claus in a black Maya *guayaberra* with white embroidery down the front as if to take the white beard look all the way down his shirt.

The bride and groom are attired to have this wedding anywhere in the world, he in a fine black suit and she in a beautiful long white gown with a veil trailing eight or ten feet behind her.

A boombox generated the music for the processional and the one hymn sung. There was no organ or piano. In this culture, this was their second wedding. Not their second marriage, just their second wedding. In the separation of church and state here, they do not honor one another's weddings. Last week was the civil ceremony to satisfy the government, and tonight would honor the wishes of their God. Someone arranged for a video camera, a rental I am sure. Every one of the one hundred and twenty would be in the video several times before the evening was over.

The minister alternated several times between New Testament scripture reading, personal advice, and instruction on the meaning of these scriptures for a young married couple. Someone once told me that words were the currency of academe; it is also true of the protestant Christian ministry in this place.

The little children are amazingly quiet and content in the still, heavy air of a humid summer evening in the jungle. I have been accustomed to them climbing over church pews and running up and down the aisles at Catholic masses that I have attended for other weddings or baptisms or *quincieras* (sweet sixteen coming out parties only at fifteen).

The groom and bride were pronounced man and wife and they turned to face the one hundred and twenty caring friends and family. Parents, grandparents, and others quickly traded places alongside the newlyweds for photos for the handful of people that had small Kodaks. The "photo shoot" was over in a matter of minutes.

Typically, the reception was to be held in the municipal building hall. We walked the few blocks down to and through the village square and into the hall. How could I have driven when even the bride and groom had to walk? Tables were set around a center dance floor for two hundred and fifty guests. That was a lot of food and beverage to provide in an economy where four dollars was the minimum wage…and that is a day, not an hour! It was now three hours after my mealtime, and my stomach is of the belief that having gone through the receiving line, hugging and kissing the groom and bride, respectively, that I am entitled to sit and eat while the while the other guests go through the receiving line. I lost that vote 249-1! I was sure that I would get the little kids votes, but they are still content and sit quietly, waiting patiently for the right and proper times for things.

We all believe that they make a very attractive couple. Then again, I don't believe that I have ever seen or heard report of a newlywed couple that wasn't attractive at their wedding, as in, "I am sure that their children will have nice personalities."

We will be entertained by *Charly y Sus Teclados*, "Charley and his keyboard." The receiving line ended and the dance floor was cleared for the newlyweds to do the appropriate dance of…"The New Married Guys Waltz" or whatever the correct title might be. Charly began to touch his *teclados* and the newlyweds began to sway back and forth. The groom showed me that alternating your weight from foot to foot, turning a little with each weight change, and stepping ever so slightly on her beautiful gown, qualified as dancing. I have much to learn in this regard.

As is the custom in this culture, the tables have favors for the guests to take with them as they leave. This night we had wooden *servietas*, napkin holders, hand cut, glued, and painted. I will soon be putting an addition on my house to store the assortment of *servietas* that I have amassed over many years of weddings, baptisms, and *quinciearas*. We also had a piece of green florist foam encased in various lengths of Popsicle sticks in what could be Chinese in design. An artificial white rose and green leaves rise up out of the green foam. There were also rather attractive candlesticks, white with white candles and white ribbons inscribed with "Oscar and Silvia," our newlyweds. It strikes me that either a lack of financial resources encourages creativity or that financial resources dull creativity. The table favors are beautiful and special in this way.

Charly started to sing along with the *teclado* touching. This night I was smart enough to find seating as far away from the speakers as possible, and the indications were that I would avoid any pain in my ears this evening.

It must be some Maya law about wedding, baptism, or *quinciera* reception food. There must always be the cold carrot, potato, and green pea salad, a chicken salad or mock chicken salad type sandwich wrapped in a napkin, and the dreaded tamale. This night there was also something that appeared to be a Mc Donald's Apple Pie. Further investigation proved that the McDonald's apple pie look-alike was actually a deep-fried and sugared turkey taco, if you can imagine. If you can, it makes imagining the Santa Claus in a black *guayaberra* a bit easier.

This is a religiously conservative wedding reception, which presents two prospects. One, the *cerveza* will not be flowing and two, as a result, we may get home before breakfast.

Cinderella's carriage would soon revert to vegetable status, all had finished eating, and the wee ones were still totally content to sit and watch the goings on. This and the deep fried and sugared turkey taco were amazing me.

The music seemed quite familiar to me. Probably as a result of another Maya law found right after the one about food. To the rhythm of electronic percussion, a four bar melody is tecladoed over and over again for about twelve to fifteen minutes. Then Charly would garble something loudly and unintelligibly in into the microphone and proceed to do another twelve to fifteen minutes pretending that is was different than the previous offerings.

The bride and groom would dance again. Soon others would cut in and dance with them. Eventually many couples, spouses, and sweethearts were dancing all over the dance floor. This scene could be found in almost any town, city, country, and language. Most people are dancing like the newlyweds, gently swaying back and forth. Some swayed a little more than others, some shifted from foot to foot far more often then the electronic percussion rhythm gave the beat to do so, and others seemed totally oblivious to the rhythms beat out consistently.

Then something strange happened. The music stayed the same, but for no apparent reason, everyone on the dance floor picked up the pace. Suddenly two elderly, wrinkled, grandmotherish Maya women with colorfully embroidered white huipils, knit shawl and all, started dancing, practically jitterbugging, together. If you can imagine this, you had no problem with Santa Claus in a black *guayaberra* or the deep-fried and sugared turkey taco.

Except for the parts obviously Maya, all of this could have been found in Paris, London, Rome, New York, Chicago, or "Saturday Night in Toledo, Ohio", thank you John Denver. This night, however, was a Sunday night in Sotuto, Yucatán.

🐚 18 🐚

Hospital O'Horan

Hospital O'Horan is on the west side of town not far from the zoo on Avenida Itzaes ("it–zeyez"), which is the plural of Itza, as in ancient Maya city Chichen Itza, which means the mouth of the well of the Itza tribe of the Maya. None of this is germane to anything, but sometimes I just can't stand knowing something and not telling someone about it.

O'Horan ("oar–on") is the poorest, busiest, most hectic, and most bureaucratic hospital in Merida. I have just finished hosting a group of nursing students from North Carolina on a tour of medical facilities and services here. It is obvious the O'Horan is at the bottom of the medical totem pole…to the naked eye. I will return to this point. Medical services in Mexico are pretty much organized and delivered on the ability to pay. It ranges from rural state-run clinics where they may still be paying the bill with chickens (I don't know, but it wouldn't surprise me) all the way to facilities for those with health insurance that rival the finest hospitals in the States. In fact, I personally have never been treated in a hospital with such high technology and modern facilities. In between are levels, again, based on the ability to pay.

Here is a sad commentary; there is a relatively new hospital on the outskirts of town, a pediatric hospital that is geared to serve lower middle class families. It is curiously a joint venture between the Mexican and Korean governments: in English, The Mexico-Korea Friendship Hospital. There are people from the wealthiest neighborhoods in Merida who drive their Land Rovers and Jaguars, park them on the highway instead of the parking lot, and walk in from the highway like they just got off of a bus with the lower income families, just to try to get the lower cost services! Sometimes rich people really irritate me!

Let's get back to O'Horan. Hospital O'Horan is geared to serve the poorest of the poor. The poorest of the poor, of course, are the rural indigenous Maya. O'Horan is the most crowded, most understaffed, and poorest-equipped hospital in Merida. How bad is it!? I would like to share this story with you.

Eight or so years ago (I don't keep track of dates and events, nor do I ever remember what I or anyone else was wearing that day or what I had to eat at that restaurant. My mind is full of important things like batting averages of the Chicago White Sox, past and present.), a friend of mine had a granddaughter who needed open-heart surgery. The granddaughter was a toddler, maybe two or three years old. My friend and her family are indigenous and lived in a village about two hours east of the city of Merida. They lived off the land, an agrarian self-sufficient lifestyle. In that lifestyle, there is no such thing as money for health insurance, so using a high quality hospital for the surgery was not an option. They worked the land instead of drawing a paycheck, so they had no claim to socialized medical services through payroll deductions. They were destined to seek medical services at the hospital for the poorest of the poor, Hospital O'Horan.

If you ever had any doubt as to whether or not Mexico was a third world country, visit Hospital O'Horan. The place and its contents are worn down, if not broken down. It is teeming with humanity scurrying about in all directions. It is just wall-to-wall short, brown, indigenous people. A place like Hospital O'Horan cannot afford frills, so there are none. I'm talking about frills, frivolous things like waiting rooms or public cafeterias. If someone becomes a patient at Hospital O'Horan, this is how it works. The patient gets two visitor passes to give to family members and/ or friends. The hospital provides basically nothing to the patient outside of medical services. If you brought things into the hospital like diapers for the toddler or a change of clothing or a snack for momma and the baby, odds are that it will all end up missing. So, somebody needs to park themselves in a plastic chair just outside the visitor entrance and guard the stuff, in this case, stuff that a toddler and a mother might need for the next few days.

My friend is Doña Piedad. Everything about her—her appearance, her demeanor, her clothing, her view of life—is classic Maya. She is the queen of her realm in the village. She is intelligent, talented, and knowledgeable, highly regarded, and has one of the quickest and most infectious laughs that I have ever heard. She accompanied her daughter and granddaughter to Merida and Hospital O'Horan. Other *gringo* friends had provided the transportation to the hospital and were making sure that the family was having its needs met. Unfortunately, they had to return to the States before the surgery and asked my sweet wife and me to step in and care for the family. I lived too close to Norwegians for a while so I replied, "Ya sure, you betcha."

The next morning, we went to Hospital O'Horan to check on Doña Piedad. The front of Hospital O'Horan is ground level but for some reason, the side entrance for visitors to see patients is a fifty stair climb over a 100 yard span. The stairs themselves were thirty yards wide. It looked more like a Chicago museum entrance. When you get to the top, all you can see is indigenous women, most of them dressed in the traditional *huipil*, a white dress with bright colors embroidered along the hem and neckline. They were probably fifty to seventy-five women sitting in plastic chairs, visiting in small groups or moving back and forth to and from the entrance. There are low murmurs, but it is relatively quiet. It was hard to spot Doña Piedad; nearly everyone was in white, had gold in their teeth, with a shawl, 4'8" tall, a little chubby, a complexion of clove and cinnamon, and jet black hair. We tried to blend in! We received a lot of stares because we were obviously not poor enough to use this hospital. We finally spotted Doña Piedad.

The surgery had been delayed earlier in the week because the little girl had a cold. Today it was delayed because there were no empty beds in the recovery room. So for a few days, momma sits upstairs in the hospital with the toddler, and grandma sits in a plastic chair guarding the stuff. Maybe tomorrow is the word from the hospital. Doña Piedad even slept overnight in the plastic chair. She eats from the vendors in the street on the side of the hospital. We checked with Doña Piedad about any needs and she gave us two or three items. We went to a supermarket not far from the hospital and returned to the stares of the Maya women about an hour later. This routine went on for a couple of days. The other Maya women were amazed. "Doña Piedad, our people clean houses and cook for rich people. How do you get rich *gringos* working for you?" Doña Piedad is coy. "Oh, I have known them for years." She would explain no more than that.

Finally the day arrives. The baby is healthy and there is space in the recovery room. The surgery takes place. One by one all the family members come by to express their concern and support. It was a solemn day full of both hopes and fears. After a few hours of waiting, the doctor came out and said that the surgery went well and that the little girl would be fine. She was resting now. We left the hospital and returned the next morning. During that evening, we talked about the reality that Doña Piedad never, to our knowledge, went into the hospital to see her granddaughter. I surmised that she probably had never been in a multi-story building and was afraid and too proud to ask for help. Every day that we visited she would give my wife the pass and tell her to go and check on things. She would always refuse when we encouraged her to go in. The next morning we pushed the issue with her and, sure enough, she was afraid of getting lost in the big building. If she went into a room with many doors, how would she know which one to use to get out? Doña Piedad agreed to go in if the watchman would let my wife accompany her and show her where everything is. They approached the watchman and he, of course, denied their request. Doña Piedad broke down and cried and told the watchman that her granddaughter was very ill and that she may never see her granddaughter alive again. "Ok, the two of you go in!" The watchman relented and let them in just to get this pitiful scene away from his watch.

While my wife and Doña Piedad were in the hospital, there I was sitting in a plastic chair outside of this massive concrete structure guarding the stuff in the middle of seventy-five Maya women. I was trying hard to blend in and failing miserably. They began to gather around and hover over me and bombard me with questions all at once. I have trouble understanding one person in Spanish, let alone several voices at once. I put on a fake smile and tried to nod and acknowledge each one. I didn't know what else I could do at the moment. I wasn't real sure if the stuff was safe; they might start going through the bags and then what would I do? Should I line up the bags and throw myself over them? Surely they would not try to pick up a 250-pound *gringo* off of the bags just to get some diapers. Then I remembered something. I had brought some photographs with me in case there was a lull in the conversation with Doña Piedad. "*¿Quieres ver nieve?* Do you want to see snow?" "*¡Nieve!*" they shouted. "*¡Sí, sí!*" I had pictures of a recent snow storm in Iowa. I passed out the photos to a chorus of ooohs and ahhhhs. After a few minutes they gave the photos back, and I quietly explained that I had been visiting the village Tinum for many years and that Doña Piedad and her family were friends of mine. They nodded and returned to their plastic chairs and left me in peace to guard the bags of stuff. When my wife and Doña Piedad came out of the hospital, they were both laughing loudly. "What is happening?" "Doña Piedad deserves an Oscar. Her crying was all an act; she pulled one over on these smart alec city folks!"

The next day Doña Piedad went up into the hospital to see her daughter and granddaughter and came back out beaming. "*¡Ella brinca en la cama!* She is jumping up and down on the bed!" One day after surgery she was jumping on the bed! Do you believe in miracles yet? The following morning the little girl could be released as soon as the family paid the bill. The facility was free from the state, the nurses were paid by the state, and the surgeon volunteered his services. All that was to be paid for was about twenty dollars worth of bandages and baby aspirin. The prevailing opinion around Merida is that Hospital O'Horan is a pretty bad place. My Maya friends would disagree. Hospital O'Horan just saved a little girl's life and made her whole for the first time in her life for twenty dollars. To my Maya friends, Hospital O'Horan is a blessing.

Footnote:

I drove my white VW Jetta to the hospital door and my sweet wife, Doña Piedad, and her daughter and granddaughter piled in, and we started our two hour drive to the village. Doña Piedad calls my Jetta the white rocket because of the way I drive. Once at the village, we dropped them off at their *na* ("hut") and went over to the *na* of friends who let us use it when we visit. Doña Piedad said that she would make us anything that we wanted for breakfast the next morning. "*Polcanes*," we cried. A *polcan* is a snakehead in Maya and is called that because of its shape. It is a little like a hush puppy, but filled with white beans and onions. While we were enjoying our *polcanes*, Doña Piedad was making the thickest tortilla I had ever seen, so thick in fact that she was rolling them on their sides to cook the edges. "What is that for, Doña Piedad?" "After eating those AWFUL city street tortillas for a week, this is just for ME!"

🐉 **19** 🐚

Irving

We said goodbye to Irving this morning nearly eight years to the day since Irving came into our lives. It is an easy time to remember because this morning and eight years ago were the days following the world cup. I spent many a year being totally unaware of the world cup. Oh, occasionally I would see some newsreel (Do we still use newsreel in this day and age?) about a game in some far away country against a relatively unknown country and after several hours of running around without any hand-to-eye coordination (they did everything with their feet), somebody would accidentally kick the ball behind some guy in a totally different color uniform than anyone else and they would all quit and go home. The fans in the overcrowded stadiums, probably overcrowded because they were in a town with absolutely nothing else to do, like Manchester on the Whippett or Rio de Clinique., were always so irritated that it took the entire afternoon or evening for anyone to score that they expressed their frustrations by beating the stuffing out of each other. It was also possible that they were anticipating that the pot roast that they put into the oven before the game was now burned to a crisp. They would have settled for just shouting insults and a few profanities but their voices were shot from having sung some stupid athletic club fight song for several hours. Not completely sated with the stuffing beating over hours of poor athletic prowess, they would then turn their frustration on local law enforcement by showering them with empty beverage containers and used Popsicle sticks. They turn the cameras on just as local law enforcement looks at the crowd like they have never seen anything like this before and are completely baffled why they are so upset. All of this impacts American foreign policy and aid as we use this phenomenon as criteria for just who in the world should we take into our confidence as a colleague in industrial and first world leadership. Thus endeth today's reading, *la palabra de Dios*.

Eight years ago, the country that I was located in still had a team playing in the world cup. The way that you could tell is that the streets were virtually empty, and we could have robbed every store in town to a state of emptiness as all the employees and owners were in the back with their eyes glued to television sets. Most people, if they are as good looking and overflowing with common sense as I am, detest car shopping because of the nature and frequency of encounters with salesman. Eight years ago on this day in Mexico, you could check out every used and new car in the city without being bothered by a salesman. If you actually wanted to buy a car, you had a problem.

All of this Eden ended when all of a sudden the streets were full of cars with horns honking, beverages being consumed, and people screaming while leaning more than halfway out of moving vehicles and waving Mexican flags the size of Kate Smith's undergarments. At the Monument to the Country, the main thoroughfare was in total gridlock. I have always maintained that my preference when in a foreign country was to appear as a total geek tourist rather than a sojourner in their land, so the opportunity could not be passed up, we HAD to ask what was happening. I rolled up my pants cuffs an extra two inches to display my white socks worn with sandals and stuck a pocket protector in my shirt to look right for the moment. "Mexico just tied Holland in the World Cup," was our answer. Tied? Tied !!! Tied%@#*(&^$!%. If this country had come to a screeching halt over a tie, what on earth would they do with a victory? Fortunately, we may never know.

The search for Irving had been an easy decision. We were furnishing our home in Yucatán and were taking the busses and buying things like six ceiling fans and bringing them home. Did you ever try to carry six ceiling fans onto and off of a bus? You have to hunker down real low and sit with your legs real close together or you have to pay for an extra seat. We started the search by walking to used car lots in the summer jungle heat in mid-July. Oh, did I forget to tell you that Irving was a car? Silly me! You see, vehicles in Latin America are named, like in all those low budget films with overcrowded busses flying around on third world dirt road always have some sweetheart's name or tribute to Jesus written across the windshield. We were looking for a car and in the end, the name was Irving. It didn't take much consideration after hoofing it to the first lot to decide that in the jungle heat, it may be wise to rent a car to facilitate finding a car. For the most part it was an uneventful day. We visited lot after lot without discussion with any sales personnel as they were all inside a small shanty with air conditioning watching the World Cup. We saw a plethora of used vehicles sitting in 110 degrees, closed up with a few years of cigarette smoke in the upholstery becoming more and more pungent as the sun rose in the sky. We were not encouraged. We finally ended up at a VW dealer not far from our house where we found a brand new stripped-down VW Jetta with nothing extra but air conditioning was less expensive while on sale than a used Jetta with all the extras. This was a no brainer, so we purchased the new all white 1998 Jetta. Why a Jetta? Because, inch for inch, a Jetta had a larger *cahuela* than other makes and models and a large *cahuela* ("trunk") was important for hauling suitcases back and forth to the airport.

Now we faced the daunting task of blending into the culture by naming the Jetta. Neither my sweet wife nor I were inclined to put names of girlfriends on the windshield and were a bit too mainstream Protestant to splash a Jesus oriented message on it. Friends had already taken *Blanca Nieva* ("Snow White") for their VW, and Polar Bear seemed too much for a VW. We mused over our experiences of the past day or two and came to realize that it had been an unusual day or two for Hispanic names. Our neighbors Rudolfo and Carolina just had a baby boy and named him Kevin Ceballos. The car that we rented to go car shopping was rented from a fellow named Williams Gonzales, and the VW salesman was named Irving Fuentes. Obviously we didn't need a Hispanic name here in Yucatán, so we agreed on "Irving." We did not, however, have "Irving" etched in Gothic font across the windshield.

The last trip with Irving was to the site of the World Cup traffic gridlock at the monument to the country. It was early in the morning, and I needed a photo of the monument without traffic. We turned the keys over to a friend who would be selling Irving for us, and we headed to the airport for our return to the states.

On the plane, I began to reflect on all the places Irving and I had been together. I have written about several experiences in Yucatán, and Irving had taken me to nearly all of them…and back. Irving and I have been to the remote corners of the Yucatán peninsula, Kohunlich and Chetumal near Belize, Kalakmul Reserve near the Guatemala border, Edzna in Campeche to the west, Isla Holbox to the north, and all up and down the Caribbean coast of Quintana Roo, including multiple trips down the road to hell to Punta Allen. One trip to Punta Allen included loaning Irving to a wedding so that the bride could be paraded around the three block by eight block island in style. The cute young thing that requested using Irving assured me the she new how to drive, but apparently she had never driven a car where you had to release the brake. All in our party were invited to the wedding celebration in exchange for Irving, so we all went in our wrinkled shorts, T-shirts, and sandals! It didn't matter to these gracious people. What I remember about the reception and celebration was that I could smell Irving coming because of the burning of the brakes! As it turned out, there was no damage to Irving. On another trip to Punta Allen, I misjudged a large bovine-sized pothole and landed so hard that it cut Irving's gas line. I could actually see the gas needle moving to the left towards the ominous "E" icon, which did not stand for "Enough Already!" Irving and I shortened the remainder of the trip by speeding up and trying to take the huge potholes by being airborne rather than slowly and carefully driving down into and out of potholes almost as big as Irving. We were trying to reach Punta Allen before we ran out of gas and were stranded on the twenty six miles of jungle terrain void of civilization. Irving was fantastic, flying nimbly through the air while I displayed considerable angst, if not outright fear. Irving spit and sputtered and came to a halt right at the Army barracks at the edge of Punta Allen. All I had left to do was walk eight short blocks down a sandy lane to my friends home. "E" really did mean "enough," driving that is.

Irving has carried the sands of the Caribbean and the western and northern Gulf of Mexico beaches. He has worn mud back and forth from some of the greatest ancient Maya cities half covered with jungle vegetation. Irving has carried university presidents, educators, dignitaries, brides, Maya children on their very first car ride, friends, my children, my grandchildren, and my mother. Irving has transported ceiling fans, huge pots and plants, Maya village artifacts, but most of all Irving has carried memories for me my wife and countless others that have shared Yucatán with us.

Yesterday, I took Irving for his last gentle caring hand wash, he has been too special to be put through a heartless machine. He was meticulously cleaned inside and out by someone who took great pride in his work. You know, Irving always ran better when he was clean. We drove over to a friend's house and gave my friend the keys.

Goodbye, Irving.

P.S. Irving was sold in less than one week later to a young family that only drove him back and forth to church on Sundays, and the children never put their shoes on the backs of the front seats. A nice man wipes the dust off of him every day and never gives him cheap gas.

20

A Man, a Child, and a Bee:
A Report on Hurrican Isadore

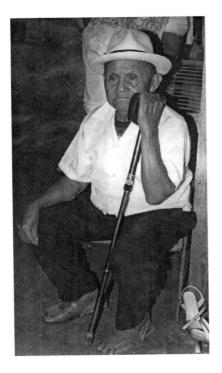

This is a man from Seye, Yucatan. I have never known his name; he is always just called "Abuelo", grandfather. This photo was taken about three years ago at the party for the 1st birthday for his great-grandson, Angel.

I visited him again just recently. He had changed so much since the photo was taken. Possibly some of the changes are due to an additional three years of wear and tear on his already eighty-something body. Possibly the changes are a result of not being able to reconcile why God or the gods would cause or permit the fury and power of a major hurricane to rip through his home, his village, his family, and his life.

The sparkle is gone now from his eyes, but not just the sparkle, since he cannot see well anymore either. He believes that his glasses have quit working. His cane doesn't support him now the way it used to. Instead, there is a rope strung through the length of the one and only room in his home, a *na*, Mayan for a hut made of thatch and sticks. He hangs onto the rope with both hands to move about the *na*.

The hurricane didn't take away the roof of his *na* as it did to so many other *naob* throughout the Yucatán. Somehow, I am not sure how, the hurricane lowered his roof so that it now was an overhang over the doorways. I had to nearly double over to enter the *na*. There were holes all about the roof, not finger-sized holes but basketball-sized holes. On this day the holes let a lot of bright sunshine into the *na*. His family wants him to leave the *na*, but he refuses: after all, it is his home, where he belongs.

Despite his weakened condition, the memories of the horror of the hurricane, and the bleak future, he rose to greet us as we entered. He extended his hand in friendship and smiled often as we chatted. I think that I caught a glimpse of the old sparkle every now and then.

He was full of dignity, warmth, and hospitality. I must remember this man when the day comes when some of my abilities leave me, or life deals me an unjustified cruel blow.

Nicte Ha ("Nick–tay Hah"), Mayan for water lily, was

maybe five years old when I first met her. I have always though that she was as pretty as her name. She is from the village of Kopoma in Yucatan. Somewhere time has flown by, and I am approaching Abuelo's age. The photo you see is Nicte Ha at her *quinceañera*, a sweet-sixteen-type coming out party but at fifteen years old in this culture.

Nicte Ha has changed from a little girl to a beautiful young woman overnight. She too experienced the hurricane. She was more fortunate than many as her relatively well-off family had a house of concrete block to protect her. Her father is a bilingual, Spanish and Mayan, schoolteacher in the village. She told us of her family huddling together in the house during the wind and rain. She said the hurricane made a deafening high-pitched whistle sound as it passed. She spoke of the changes in the amount of light filtering through the cracks in the doorway: first the darkness that accompanied the fury, the bright light as the eye of the hurricane passed over, and then darkness again as the backside of the storm beat down upon the house.

She told of people up in trees to avoid the rising waters, clutching the tree with one arm and a baby in the other. She still trembled as she shared stories of neighbors and friends in coastal villages, the villages hardest hit. She shared stories more gruesome and frightening than I care to relate. I must remember Nicte Ha when I think that the bumps and bruises in my life are serious.

These are but two of the hundreds of thousands of lives damaged by the hurricane, some much more than others. But for nearly all, *hay vida*, there is life, albeit life that will never forget the day of the hurricane. Actually, it was days of hurricane followed by the seemingly never ending rains that uprooted entire citrus orchards, washed away the family farm, sent fishing boats flying into oblivion, felled huge trees and concrete street lamps and drowned the cattle and poultry. Now, life is being reconstructed one piece and one day at a time. Lives that are being built back up with dignity, faith, gratitude, and love. I must remember these lives.

A Bee

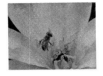 The newspapers and television stations didn't report everything about the effects of the hurricane. They dealt mainly with human, huge trees, and large animal tragedies. The reality is that everything was affected, but much went unnoticed. No one reported on the plight of the honeybee. I care because the honeybee of Yucatan is my favorite species of bee:

stingless! Can I really take a bee seriously?

When the hurricane blew down the big old trees into the floodwaters, many bees lost their homes in the holes in the trees. Even if they weren't blown down, the holes filled with water, and the bees lost their homes. Can I take the plight of a homeless bee seriously?

The floodwaters from the hurricane and following rains killed all the small yellow flowers that dot the landscape this time of year, depriving the bees of a food and pollen source. The next flowering season will be springtime. Some people made a bee food for a while from the peels of oranges, but when the floodwaters loosened the roots of the orange trees and sent them down into the water, the oranges rotted and again there was no food for the bees. Can a hungry bee be a serious thing?

It is if you harvest honey and take it to market in order to buy food and clothing for your children or harvest crops pollinated by the bees.

21

A Journey on the Yucatán Express

August 2002, I am theoretically in the jungle. I am, but also in a city. It is a city pushing a million people during the day with labor coming in from the pure indigenous villages surrounding the city and the tourists interested in archeology and temples and pyramids and lost cities in the jungle. Step outside the city, and the short, stubby jungle of Yucatán surrounds in all directions. I am on maybe my fourth or fifth *Cuba Libre* sin Coca of the evening, I can't handle *Cuba Libres* with Coca Cola in them, can't sleep with the carbonization and caffeine, so I trade the Coca Cola for more rum. I can't remember the day: was it spent in the old Spanish colonial downtown, or thirty minutes north at the beaches of the Gulf of Mexico, or did I just return from another retreat in a sleepy Maya fishing village on the Caribbean coast with a quiet sandy beach lined with palm trees and a bay with the second longest barrier reef in the world? I don't know, but I am settling down with the newspaper El Diario de Yucatán. There is an article the Diario about a new cruise/ferry service that was going to provide cruise/ferry service between Tampa and Progreso. I was not particularly enthused because I have no need to ferry a car as I have vehicles in both countries. However, I kept the article and tried to stay in touch with the progress as I have friends who talk about driving here and this would excite them.

    I am a Midwesterner and I am not sure if this is a ferry or a cruise or even if it is a boat or a ship. I have caught blue gill, perch, and small mouth bass from a boat and water skied behind one too, so this must be a ship. I have no point of reference for the ferry/cruise issue. I also am usually in such an emotional hurry to get here that thirty-six hours on the open water rather than a few hours of connecting flights is unthinkable.

The autumn months are spent each year in the good ol' USA, totally enveloped in the season of college football, following my favorite college team wherever they may be playing. My equally enthusiastic spouse and I have had a lot of interesting and fun trips this way. Sometime between games and travel planning, I started checking out my return to Yucatán: i.e., planes flights, costs, dates, and stuff. After 9/11, the airline industry in the good ol' USA made a lot of noise about encouraging Americans to fly again. I don't know how they imagined doing that but it certainly wasn't through pricing. The cost to fly to Yucatán skyrocketed. Maybe the price inducements were from Boston to Boise or something, but the rest of us were paying much higher prices. In the meantime, my friends were salivating at the prospect of a service from Tampa to Progreso. Reacting to their fervor, I checked into the ship thing. I found that I could actually fly to Tampa, pay for taxis, the ship, etc., and it would cost considerably less than flying all the way to Yucatán. Being fundamentally frugal by nature and not bound by time constraints, I decided to give the ferry/cruise thing a look-see.

The first obstacle was to get over the diametric opposition of the name Yucatán Express. I am too young to remember The Orient Express but I understand that it was mysterious and frightening, and wasn't it a train? Also, doesn't "express" mean *rapido* or some kind of PDQ? It strikes me that the Yucatán Express takes 2,160 minutes to cross the Gulf of Mexico while a plane covers the same distance in exactly 105 minutes, more or less. So how does twenty times slower qualify as "express"? Possibly we aren't to consider this in real time but rather in attitudinal time. Maybe instead of rising early in the day and rushing to the airport two hours ahead of departure only to wait in long lines, and then wait an a overlit noisy area seeing and hearing a zillion or so others racing back and forth to take their turns waiting in lines, and then at the last minute rush into the jet and strap yourself into a seat without space for your knees, wait until the flight attendants can almost walk upright and serve you a bag of pretzels (they have done away with the cardboard flavored meals on most flights), suffer through the delay in departure caused by my inexperienced folk who spend forever trying to cram five cubic feet of their personal stuff into a three cubic feet receptacle and failing to understand that until they themselves sit down and strap themselves in like the rest of us, this baby ain't moving! Being delayed by a reenactment of "Ma and Pa Kettle Ride the Silver Bird," we are now setting 18th in line for takeoff, but once we are airborne it is only 105 minutes of flight time. We are not considering the time to taxi to the terminal; for example, I am convinced that American Airlines lands most of their Dallas flights in Oklahoma then taxi down to Dallas. Once we get unstrapped and inside the terminal, we can walk for two or three miles (which pleases our doctors as it gets the heart rate up) and wait again for our luggage to arrive, which by the way was getting off the plane before we were and rode, not walked, to the baggage collection area!

    With the Express, however, we just saunter onto the ship, have a few drinks, listen to some music, never strap ourselves in, and never have to sit down if we don't want to. Pretty soon the ship begins to move, we have a sumptuous meal, get distracted by some entertainment and fall asleep to the gentle roll of the waves. We wake in the morning, do last night all over again all day, and someone else makes up the bed. All in all, 2,160 minutes fly by and we arrive refreshed bright and early in the morning ready to start a day rather than exhausted and grumpy at the end of a day ready to call it quits. My preference became clear to me. I checked out the web site and called the 1-800 number and ordered our tickets for the Yucatán Express.

    The Good Dr. Van Bodegraven Ma'am and I arrived at terminal 7 in Tampa quite early, as our plane into Tampa was an early flight. We wondered if arriving so early would leave us sitting on an empty pier by ourselves for a few hours. Not so, the terminal was open, the baggage handlers were eager to take our bags to the screening conveyor for their first tips of the day. We were served immediately and got our boarding passes and meal vouchers. Now we could just hang around for a while and assess the other passengers as they arrive.

It readily seemed obvious that this crowd was ready for transportation, not a Pacific Princess experience. I doubt if any of them brought a suit and tie or tuxedo in case they were invited to sit at the Captain's table for dinner. In fact, we never saw a captain. Once in a while a fellow with bars on the shoulders of his white shirt and a vague resemblance to Commander Whitehead appeared, but I don't believe that he was the Captain. Before long, those who brought their cars were summoned to begin loading the cars, and shortly we were invited to board. I didn't really know what to expect. I have seen a lot of things look much better than reality in color glossy brochures, and one reality is that I reserved a room with a private toilet above a floating car carrier. I have always held the belief that ralphing during high seas and bad weather is not a communal activity.

As we entered the ship or soon thereafter, we were offered the drink of the day. The drink can vary each day but it must contain rum, something fruity, and have a Chinese-made paper umbrella stuck in it to be considered for the drink of the day. For an extra $49.95 or maybe less than that, you can keep the souvenir glass. Leaning more toward trying to project a John Wayne persona, I passed on the umbrella drink; someone else in our group of two didn't pass on the offer, so now we have a complete set of one glass for our dining room buffet at home.

I will relate this now, and it should be repeated at least another twenty-seven times throughout my ramblings here, but it won't be: The staff, ALL the staff, was very attentive, patient, excellently trained, and performed wonderfully throughout the voyage!

Delmer was our room steward. He explained that the only thing that opened in the room was the toilet and that the showers were down the hall. He gave us his cleaning hours so we could plan around it. Delmar has a great smile.

Our room (or is it a cabin on a ship?) was very clean and neat. In a cabin, no matter where you stand or sit you are in someone else's way. It was designed and decorated in a way that encourages one to leave it for plush surroundings like the casino, lounge, or restaurant. So we left.

Everything on the ship was easily accessible via a maze of narrow passageways and highly polished brass railings and carpeted staircases leading to more long narrow passageways that eventually take you to someplace that looks like everyplace else...except the outer decks, they look different. P.S. The outer decks that I tried didn't go all the way around the ship unless you wanted to help change a large bearing or something.

Why are there so many bells and gongs and such in a casino? Do they make people feel better about parting with their hard-earned money?

The Dolphin Lounge was a very nice room set up for lounging, of course, and for entertainment. Island Breeze, a Caribbean-style musical group consisting of Virgin Islander Alvin, his rhythm-making machine, and keyboard, began playing before departure. It is easy to talk over Alvin; his music is soft and gentle. If you do talk over him, however, you will miss the subtle humor of the songs he blends together and how he changes some lyrics of classical Caribbean tunes to reflect on his fellow staff.

We met Diane from Canada; actually, the ship is crawling with Canadians as many of them winter in the vacant Yucatecan beach houses along the Gulf of Mexico coast. We met Lynn, too, whose father worked with Diane or something like that but they had never met before. Lynn is actually a new staff member and is learning the ropes this trip. Somewhere on the ship is someone from a university that I interviewed at earlier in the week. I keep an eagle eye out for some sign that will tip me off as to who they are. A polo shirt with the university name on it would be nice!

A family seated near us nodded and then the father said that he remembered me from a few years ago when they were driving their car in Merida, and I commented that I didn't believe that they drove down all the way from Pennsylvania. I remember such an occurrence but it was with a car from Georgia. I am embarrassed that I don't remember this average, pleasant-looking family. How can he remember me...is it because I look like Burl Ives's head attached to a bowling ball? They, Randy and Kathy, are living and doing mission work in Yucatán. They brought down over a ton of clothing for Hurricane Isadore victims. We also brought down a large suitcase of clothing for a particular village we associate with. It's not a ton, but hey, I'm not in mission work. I am into checking out new restaurants and having *Cuba Libres sin Coca*.

The ship departed Tampa on time, and many of us sat at the front of the lounge watching the harbor go by until we were completely surrounded by the Gulf of Mexico. The ship moved, not just across or through the water, but in the water. The ship is capable of dipping unannounced either left, right, front, or back without any particular rhythm. I repeat, I am from the Midwest, so I don't use starboard, aft, stern, and port. Left, right, front, back works for me. The front, by reason, would be the pointy part to cut through the water. Aft or stern give me no clues whatsoever.

I at first thought that it was my impaired sense of balance and artificial body parts that had me staggering around, trying

not to crash headlong into another passenger. I soon realized that everyone walks just like me! I planned to test the theory that a few drinks would create a counter-stagger effect, and I would look reasonably nor-

The front, pointy part of the ship, also known as DiCaprio Point. Photo by Alan Van Bodegraven

mal. It's like limping with both legs, who's to know? Curiously, it seemed that the smaller the person, i.e., children, the less trouble they had walking about, or as the Canadians say "aboot." Later I discovered that it is a considerable feat to be in the shower trying to bend over and wash between your toes without careening your cranium directly into the wall.

The show that evening after a wonderful meal was excellent. Later the strains of Yucatán Express Quartet, an international four-piece orchestra, filled the lounge. The cruise director encouraged everyone NOT to dance unless they had a whole pile of insurance as the seas were picking up, and the ship was rolling a bit too much for dancing. I, however, slept like a baby through the night to the rolling of the ship.

Morning was something else. The winds had picked up or we kept hitting whales or something. There weren't enough *Cuba Libres sin Coca* in the world to help me walk straight. (OK, if you haven't figured it out, a *Cuba Libre* is a rum and coke and means "Free Cuba." Drink as much as you will and Cuba still isn't free. It's just a gimmick to sell Coca Cola. So I order my *Cuba Libres* without Coca Cola, just rum with a lime twist since I don't intend to free Cuba, at least not this way) "Walking" to breakfast consisted of grabbing on to one railing and then lunging forward to the next one. They were awarding gold stars for your refrigerator door to anyone who could carry their food from the buffet line to their table intact. For entertainment purposes, we were given a window seat, as far as possible from the food. The red marks all over my face from when my head would go one way and my fork the other should heal within the week.

The schedule for the day was chock full of activities. Some were feasible with the movement of the ship while others were not. Although everything was free of charge, I considered trying to sell tickets to the morning yoga and line dancing classes as I envisioned the yoga participants achieving the spiritual high of the Maharishi Maheshi as they were able to levitate briefly in the yoga position. The only straight line the dancers could accomplish was sliding directly across the copper dance floor of the Dolphin Lounge on their buttocks. They also had bingo scheduled. Today it would be more like "Chips Ahoy"! Pouring in the Basic Cocktail Mixology class would be a hoot as the glass would probably move before the poured liquid arrived. Somewhat disconcerting was that scattered throughout the public areas were the small stacks of small white paper bags, you know, the kind you find in the seat pocket of the seat in front of you on the airplane that should be in the upright position.

So we avoided any physical activities by nailing the day's crossword puzzle. We then crawled over to a corner where a movie would be shown. The flick was *Kate and Leopold* with Meg Ryan and a bunch of people I never heard of. I have hardly heard of Meg Ryan. Living in the Yucatán for some recent years and a noticeable lack of cultural exposure before that has left me unaware of contemporary film, theatre, music, and new prepared foods on the market. I consider it a blessing. I'm not saying that I haven't attended a movie in quite a while, but I do miss the piano player.

Now it was just a short tumble down the stairs to the dining room.

We chatted with a woman from Minnesota now living in Telchac Puerto. We met a couple from Miami. He was a retired engineer, she grew up near our home in Merida, and we know several Yucatecos in common. We met Yucatecos returning home. There was a couple we saw often and always nodded. They walked into our favorite restaurant in Merida a couple of nights later. It was their anniversary, so we had our waiter friends deliver a bottle of wine to their table.

The dining hall was reached, miraculously. They gave up on the star system and just took the food to the tables for you. Today's luncheon was particularly exciting as the swells caused dishes to go careening off the tables crashing to the floor. "Quite a list to the starboard," I said, momentarily abandoning my midwestern nautical vocabulary, "and pass me more of that lime Jell-O so I can keep my daily calorie count down enough to afford to get snockered on some kind of rum drinks in the evening." I had pre-arranged, with pre-tip, for the wait staff to remove any Chinese-made paper umbrellas heading my way.

Ron plays piano during lunch and dinner meals. I hate Ron. We are about the same age, and he has a full head of thick wavy hair. I am seriously folliclely challenged. On the other hand, I don't hate Ron because tomorrow I will be disembarking to enjoy my beloved Yucatán, and Ron has to stay on board and play the piano while the ship causes his piano and stool to move about while he tries to play.

Ron took a shine to us, maybe because after many songs we, as we should have, applauded politely, or maybe because we were mouthing the words to many of the old Connie Francis numbers that he was playing. Maybe, actually I am out of maybes. He came over to our tables (as well as others) between sets as he did last evening and commenced to share two important items. One, he really hated ships this small. It seemed that he was not enjoying performing through the pitches and rolls. Two, we learned his life story, which was necessary to share in order that we fully appreciate his extraordinary adoration of Connie Francis. He gave my wife, free of charge, a Connie Francis tape that included many songs she recorded but were never released. For me, he gave the opportunity to buy a tape of him playing old Floyd Kramer songs. I could probably get Floyd Kramer himself at a truck stop in the $2.99 bargain tape bin, but for $10 I could get the same songs but by Ron...and autographed by Ron to boot!

Ron proclaimed that we were the best cruise ship passengers that he has ever been with, or at least on this particular cruise. I suspect that there will be several other "best-evers" until the remaining 499 copies of his tape are sold.

There was a trivial pursuit game planned. Being the best trivial pursuit players on our small block of retired tobacco farmers, we raced down, actually crawled down, to face only one opponent who dared face off against us, being local champions and all. Our opponent was not native to the culture of the good ol' U.S. of A.; we knew we had this one in the bag. It wasn't even close! Following that victory we wandered off to the Basic Mixology Class offered by Cecil the Jamaican at the casino bar. Wandering or stumbling through the casino was another reminder that this was a crowd looking for transportation, not entertainment. Cecil taught the class for just the two of us and soon ice cubes, swizzle sticks, glasses, and bottles were flying. Then the ship settled down and Cecil taught us the intricacies of two complicated, three-ingredient drinks, a Margarita and a Tequila Sunrise. We were expected to consume the results of the demonstration and shared them with Cameron, fellow bar patron. Since the class products were gratis, I felt obliged to purchase a few more to make Cecil feel appreciated. The more green Jell-O decision was looking more intuitive by the moment.

During the Cecil appreciation time we chatted with Cameron and learned that he travels around Latin America buying replicas, as he shared the view the original artifacts belong in the country of origin, and markets them in the good ol' USA. Soon we had several napkins full of names and directions for him to find towns and artisans that we were aware of in Yucatán.

The theory of balancing the ship's movements with a few drinks and creating a counter-stagger effect must be working, as everything seemed noticeably calmer now. Being this close to Mexico, we felt it wise to practice the art of siesta before attempting another dining room experience.

By dinnertime, things really did calm down. I managed to get all but one small lettuce leaf safely to my table. The food, again, was excellent. Ron seemed more exuberant and relaxed in the calmer seas. (Why is it "seas" when we are only in one and it isn't a sea at all, it's a gulf?) He played only one Connie Francis song, blew us a kiss, and went into a Christmas medley. Ron probably would like a drink with rum and fruit and the Chinese-made paper umbrellas and probably doesn't like John Wayne all that much, or Jesse Ventura for that matter. But to be fair, I doubt that John Wayne or Jesse Ventura could play the piano at a professional level while it moves on a rolling ship. Good job, Ron!

Upstairs in the Dolphin Lounge, the international four piece orchestra, The Yucatán Express, was playing "In the Mood," and I wanted so much to slide my body, artificial parts and all, briskly across the copper dance floor praying the ship would list just enough to keep me from sliding all the way into the dark briny foam below. The words of my surgeon rang in my ears: "no dancing"; he was a Baptist in addition to being my surgeon.

A fellow passenger sat by himself outside the Dolphin Lounge addressing his Christmas cards. Just where does he think he can mail those in Mexico to get them delivered sometime before Memorial Day? If he was doing that just as an activity and will carry them back home to mail them, we need to introduce him to some rum and fruit drinks with little Chinese-made paper umbrellas in them.

In about ten hours we arrive in Progreso, just a short taxi ride to our home in Merida. It will be good to be home and with old friends, many of whom are more like adopted family. This will be our fifteenth consecutive Christmas in Merida.

The ship is vibrating for some reason associated, I think, with the motors. Or maybe the rudder is smacking around a shark or two. I don't know, but I used to have to put a quarter in a machine at a cheap hotel for the same sensation.

I have seen too many "Saturday Night Live" routines. At the Dolphin Lounge, I keep expecting Bill Murray or a clone to pop out at any minute and do really bad schmoozing and sing off-key for a while.

Sleeping the second night was a repeat. I slept like a baby to the rolling seas. It settled down sometime during the impressionist's routine at the lounge. It was if the water just stopped moving, looked back at the ship and muttered, " What the heck is he doing?" and never regained full strength again. The morning would be calm. Except when a *Norte* blows in, the gulf at Progreso is always calm in the mornings and then it picks up a little movement about noon every day. You can set your watch by it. Sitting on the veranda at Capitan Marisco in Progreso with a *Cuba Libre sin Coca* is the best way to observe it.

Whenever I return to Texas, I sing at the top of my lungs Gary P. Nunn's song "Going Home With the Armadillos," the unofficial national anthem of Texas. I so wish I had such a song for Yucatán. I have been working on something like:

Oh Maya Maya Maya

I'm so glad I left Ohia

It's a work in progress; I will let you know when it is finished.

The morning of our arrival, I woke early and encouraged The Good Dr. Van Bodegraven Ma'am to join me at breakfast as soon as it opened. I wanted to have breakfast, set our bags in the hall for Delmer, and get out on deck before the morning light came. It was another wonderful dining room experience. All of

Tugboat at Progreso. Photo by Alan Van Bodegraven.

the wait staff waved and called "good bye" as we left. We went out on deck and saw nothing but the darkness of night upon the water. We chatted with others who shared our love of Yucatán. We advised first timers to try not to "do" Yucatán but to allow Yucatán to just happen to them. Yucatán for many is a near mystical, near spiritual experience. It has been continually pulling me back since my first visit fifteen years ago. The four months of college football are over for me this year, and now I am going home!

I had lost track of time. Eventually a small sliver of red appeared to the east on the horizon. It seemed to melt from one color into another, hues of reds, oranges, yellows and grays. Shortly thereafter I spotted the end of the six-kilometer long pier at Progreso, said to be the longest in the world but I really don't know. Progreso is a combination of a fishing village, beach homes for folks from Merida, and in recent years a significant port for international commerce. Today it is my port, *mi puerto,* drawing me into Yucatán.

The little tugboat came out to greet us and give the ship a little nudge if needed.

The dancers met us at the terminal, welcoming us all to Yucatán.

I was home at last, refreshed and ready for the day.

Dancers in native costumes dancing the traditional Jarana. Photo by Alan Van Bodegraven.

I need to give a thank you Yucatán Express, Delmer, Clive, Jose, Mariano, Shelley, Cecil, Tim, Rany, Scott, Maria, Lynn, Audry, Alvin, Ron, Bob, Commander Whitehead, and those whose names I can't recall… all the staff and crew. You brought me to my beloved Yucatán in high spirits. I hope that each of you at some time will experience Yucatán for it is truly, as described by Tony Cohan in his book On Mexican Time, *a place remembered not in the mind, but in the senses.*

22

XIXIM

It is winter at Xixim (She-sheem) but still warm enough to wade or swim in the gulf waters, dip in the pool, or just feel the sun on your back.

Approaching five in the afternoon, the sun begins working its way toward the western edge of the water. Winter solstice wasn't that long ago and the days are short.

Some plants blossom during the winter in this unusual semi-arid, tropical terrain. Palm trees and cactus side by side provide homes and food to animals and birds.

More than anything, it is a quiet place. One hears the buzzing of a fly several feet away, not just the chirping but also the sound of bird's wings pushing through the air...all against the ever-present background of rolling waves upon the shore.

I am waiting for the night. The endless deep blue sky of the day will become complete darkness in the night. Without artificial lights, the stars will shine brighter than ever seen before.

In the morning I hear crickets afar off, birds rustling in the bushes, and small animals moving through the low grasses. Much more can be heard than seen.

It seems as though the breeze never ceases and brings clean crisp salt air unspoiled by all the "progress" of our urban lives.

A cardinal flashes its color, bright red, among the green and beige of bush and sand, as did the flycatcher with its yellow and white a few moments earlier. It is a painting on the move, with music as the sundry collection of birds call out.

The ospreys and frigates soar majestically, if not lazily, high in the azure skies. Pelicans and cormorants are closer to the water in search of their "daily bread."

Ashore, the action picks up as orioles, tanagers, and flycatchers swoop down upon the endless supply of flying insects. The smaller songbirds dart back and forth between bushes, and the hummingbirds make their mad dashes between blossoms, changing directions without ever slowing down.

Strangely, this collection of sights and sounds together create a peace and tranquility in this place called Xixim, "little seashell," on the beach at Celestun in Yucatan.

🐌 23 🐌

The Maya

Who are the Maya? Where did they come from? Where are they now? How did they build those huge structures without the use of the wheel or beast of burden? What happened to the great Maya cities? Despite all the research by learned scholars over several decades, let me, boy bookkeeper and former treasurer of the Bluffton, Ohio, Community Nursery School be the one to tell you. We really don't know!

I have read many books (OK, so three doesn't qualify as "many") on the Maya, and I will not quote from any of them to avoid the messy footnoting, citing, ibid, opcit you need to do when you use someone else's information. This is not a thesis or a term paper; it's just some of my personal drivel. Let's get on with it.

There have been many theories and much postulating about the Maya, and most all of it has been debunked leaving us pretty much clueless. With all our knowledge of things pre-historic, pre-Colombian, and pre-other stuff and our technology, we really don't know much about the Maya. They are not the oldest civilization in Mexico. That would probably be the Olmecs around Tabasco. You think that this intellectual deficiency is embarrassing? North of Mexico City there are the ruins of the ancient city of Tenochtitlan that, as far as we can tell, pre-date any known civilization in Mexico. So, how do you think that those building were constructed? Are you getting visions of space ships? So, our lack of knowledge about the Maya isn't so bad, at least we know some stuff, and the Maya are still with us. There is a reasonable chronology with the Olmecs, Aztecs, Mixtecs, Toltecs, and Maya, to name but a few that I simply can't seem to commit to memory. Primarily because it isn't as simple as remembering dates and names. The art and architecture of these various groups show that they clearly influenced each other, but who really knows who influenced whom. Just who is the chicken and who is the egg?

This much we (a little presumptuous here, throwing myself in with the scholars) know or think pretty strongly. The Maya were and still are the indigenous people of the Yucatán Peninsula. This is a remarkable statement on its own when you consider the history and plight of indigenous peoples in most of Latin America. The peninsula covers eastern Tabasco and all of Chiapas, Campeche, Yucatán, and Quintana Roo states in Mexico as well as the countries of Belize (former British Honduras), Guatemala, and parts of Honduras and maybe El Salvador. I am somewhat geographically challenged. Findings at archeological sites demonstrate that there were well-established trade routes. An exception to all this is Cacaxtla in Tlaxcala, which has been designated as a former Maya city. It is fifty miles from Mexico City, a thousand miles from the peninsula! See, you just can't pin this stuff down. So for all that we "know", we don't know it for certain. Today, there are twenty-five different Maya languages and cultures, and I mean languages, not dialects. I don't have to cite anyone here; I read this off of a poster at a museum.

Historically, the Maya had several notable qualities. They were excellent at commerce, knew food preservation with salt mined in the Yucatán, were seafarers as they inhabited Caribbean islands and sailed to Guatemalan and Yucatecan ports, magnificent astronomers, engineers, and mathematicians. They also weave a fine hammock if I may say so myself!

Their kings were gods. They didn't just construct huge temples and other buildings, but they covered them with wonderful ornate artwork. They had ball yards and a defined ball game. As late as the 1800s, they demonstrated their ability as excellent warriors. The ball court at the ancient city of Chichen Itza is an example of their engineering. It is larger than a conventional football field and the walls are constructed so perfectly for acoustics that if you speak in a normal voice on one end of the field, you could be heard clearly on the other end. I have a friend in the construction business who assured me that with today's technology and equipment, we could not build a wall that straight. That same city has a temple that is a perfect calendar, in the sense that the temple markings for the spring equinox are accurate every year without needing a leap year. These people were geniuses.

Where did they come from? The prevailing theory is that many many years ago, before Strom Thurmond was first elected, before the first Richard Daly was mayor of Chicago, I mean a really long time ago, before Columbus even knew what a boat was, a bunch of Asians walked across the frozen Bering Straits and began peopling this hemisphere, constantly moving south until they reached the tip of Argentina. This took a few years, since they were on foot. Hundreds of thousands of pages of scholarly work has been produced on this, but I have been able to sum it up for you in less than a paragraph. I hope that you appreciate that.

To this widely-accepted theory I simply say, "Bull hockey!" Do I look like I just fell off of the turnip truck? Well, maybe I do, but I still say bull hockey. Scholars have been pulling the wool over our eyes long enough on this one. I feel like the child who was the only one who could see that the emperor was naked while every else had been conned into his having invisible clothes. (What kind of children's story has a grown man walking around naked in front of children? And we worry about the television! Other than my two favorite channels, nobody else is walking around naked on television!)

OK, listen up, you are going to learn something here. For starters, I don't believe that anyone lived on the other side of the Bering Straits in the winter. They were nomadic people and would have gone south to the Koreas for the winter and stayed in little tent parks. Asian snowbirds if you will. OK, maybe I am wrong here, but try this on. One day Nanook gets up, looks out of his window and says to his slightly bearded wife, "Hey, Mushmush, the ice is pretty thick today, whaddya say we walk to the Americas for the weekend?" "Is it any warmer over there?" "No, it's about the same only not as crowded." "Well then, OK, by all means, let's walk to the Americas" Can I be wrong again? Ok, let's go a step further.

Nanook is just outside of Fairbanks, and he puts out the word that he is leading them south to warmer climes where they can not only fish without cutting a hole in the ice, but they could actually grow things, like food, and you had materials other than ice for construction. "OK, fellas, let's herd 'em on in and move 'em on out. Hey, how come you guys aren't coming?" "Well, we kinda like it here. You know, it's a lot like Iowa in the winter but all year round. You guys go on without us, and we'll be fine." And so they went slowly southward over thousands of years peopling the hemisphere, Canada, the USA, and northern Mexico. They went through King Nanook 1, Nanook 2, etc., until they couldn't count any higher. (The portable classroom had not been invented yet as an educational tool.)

One day when they had peopled almost all the way to Mexico City, the current leader, King Ramalamadingdong, decreed, much as Roman emperors were always decreeing something, "We shall construct a building on this very site!" The people cried out in unison, "A what?" "A building", he replied. Again they cried out in unison and four part harmony, "What is a building?" "My dear dolts," the king replied, "it's like a house made of stones instead of leather, and you can't carry it around, but since you can't carry it around you can make it really big." Again the people cried out in unison, four part harmony, and a little lute music, "Why?"

Get my point. These people couldn't construct anything that didn't use buffalo hides, sticks, and a little mud here and there. It makes more sense that some Egyptians made a big Kon Tiki-type of raft, went out to sea, drank too much, got lost, and came ashore just south of Cancun. "You know, after we explore a bit, we should come back to this place and party!" Yes, Egyptians I say. Now those people knew how to construct temples and pyramids and things, they had a lot of experience. I am very open to this idea.

Well, wherever they came from, they are still here. It is generally accepted that the Maya have been here 3000 – 5000 years. I read that some carbon dating have placed the Maya on the Caribbean for 10,000 years. I read that right under "for a good time call 975-32-32" Nevertheless, whatever the time is, it is a long time in one place. It is not as long as the Australian Aborigines at 50,000 years, but still a pretty long time.

The largest group of the twenty-five different groups of Maya is the Yucatec Maya, the ones that I hang with. Today's Yucatec Maya are split into two lifestyles that live harmoniously side by side. One group has moved into the cities or commutes into the cities and work in the low-paying areas of manual labor and domestic services. The other group elects to stay in the villages and live a self-sustaining agrarian life, which also includes their spiritual life. To become citified is to lose one's spiritual life and to live outside one's language and culture. This is a serious threat for the future of the Yucatec Maya as a separate culture and people.

The Maya are a beautiful people. For me, they are the heart and soul of the Yucatán, and it is for them that I keep coming back.

24

Chelem

Friends have offered me use of their beach house in Chelem during the week while I am here in Yucatán. Those of you who have traveled these parts know that if you head straight north out of Merida, in thirty minutes you arrive at the Gulf of Mexico at the town of Progreso. If you would have turned to go west around a big lagoon, you would have come to Chelem. When it is "Oh my God" hot and humid and someone gives you a beach house, well, it is one of those moments when you are so glad that you are not as dumb as you look and you accept! My friends came out with me on Saturday, showed me how everything worked, and went back into the city. My goal is to see if I can get some creative juices flowing.

Daybreak Sunday morning on the beach is a very quiet time. The gulf is calm, gently kissing the shoreline with little five-inch waves. The waters are less variegated and bluer than the normal turquoise until the sun gets higher overhead later in the morning. I am awakened by the sound the voices of teenage boys who have come to fish off of the stone jetty. They have no real tackle, just a hook on some line and a little bait. They cast out the hook without rod and reel, with the line around one hand. They don't catch much, if anything at all.

The sun is rising to my right, east down the shoreline.

Soon a nice little boat comes very close to the shoreline in front of me, very slowly. There are five or six people aboard and one is peering off the bow intently. They seem to be following something in the water. I take my morning coffee and plastic chair out to the edge of the terraza for a better view. About then another young boy casts a circular net, about six feet wide. He pulls it in, shakes it and recasts several times around the bow. After ten minutes or so of casting, they stopped and moved on further down the beach. I suppose that means that whatever they thought that they saw will still be there when I go for my morning bob in the waves.

In the background, there is a constant low drone of boat motors. Eastward down the beach maybe a quarter of a mile is the outlet or inlet, depends on whether you are coming or going I suppose, to or from a large lagoon where there are several marinas and a naval yard. At the exit of the lagoon, there is a three-hundred-foot-long stone jetty, and the sounds of the motors echo off the stones and roll down the beach to me. One by one, the small boats disappear over the horizon.

I am out of coffee and retreat to the house for more. Even in this tranquil and relaxing environment with nothing in particular to do, I feel the need to multitask. So while the microwave is heating my next cup of instant coffee, I quickly make the bed and scratch off the special code on my new cell phone card and enter another 260 minutes of service into the phone. The microwave finishes first.

I return to my seat at terrazzo edge to find an old *pescador,* "fisherman," wading about twenty five feet off shore. He examines the waters carefully and occasionally casts his six-foot net out in front of him. He, too, seems to be catching nothing and slowly works his way westward down the beach. While watching him go, I notice that I have a neighbor. A woman three houses down is hanging hammocks on her terrazzo climbs into one of them and begins to pore over the morning paper. She is too far away to acknowledge with a "Buenos Dias." The thought of swaying in a hammock in the salty breeze is quite appealing. I might hang mine out a little later.

There is usually a bird in view. Pelicans are early risers. Some are loners, and others fly in small groups of four to six. Some like to sit quietly in the water and wait for some lunch to swim by, while others like to soar about thirty feet above the water and then in a blink of an eye dive into the water to catch their prey. Still other pelicans like to fly gracefully only a foot or so over the water, occasionally dipping their bills into the water. I believe that it was the late Ogden Nash who wrote:

"Behold the pelican, whose bill can hold more than its belly can."

In the bird world, pelicans seem ruggedly handsome to me, if you are into that sort of thing.

Cormorants, too, like to glide about a foot off the water, which puzzles me because fish don't necessarily swim in a straight line. Terns like to walk the water's edge looking for the smaller marine life. There is a small bird, as yet not identified in my trusty bird book, that darts like a swallow but is too small for a swallow. They just seem to enjoy flitting here and there. They could be a variety of flycatcher. Seagulls don't seem to at all interested in food. It is probably an evolutionary development. Over time they have learned that they don't have to pursue food, just patiently hang around the beach for a while and some tourist or little kid will show up with a bag full of stale bread pieces. Humans can be very easy to entertain.

About fifteen miles east of here, there are flamingos by the thousands, and it is all quite by accident. Along this coast line it is common for there to be shallow lagoons behind the beaches. At one such lagoon, Uymitun, Hurricane Gilbert in 1988 threw a huge amount of sea water over the beach into the lagoon. With the sea water were a gazillion or so shrimp. A flock of flamingos were making the trek from one nesting area on the west side of the peninsula to another area on the north east tip of the peninsula. While flying over the Uymitun lagoon, they spotted the new supply of shrimp and stopped for lunch and never left. It is now a major nesting area. The Yucatecan flamingos are of the very pink if not almost orange variety. It comes from their diet.

I have chosen the uniform of the day: my red swimming trunks and sun block 30 for my coco. I have made out my "honey do" list for today. You know that you are really lonely when you have to make out your own "honey do" list. Sometime over the next nine hours, I need to get into the water, take a walk along the beach, and make myself something to eat. I am sure that if I focus, I can get it all done today.

The beach here is actually about a city block wide, but they build their houses way too close to the water so it feels like there is only twenty yards of beach. Global warming and rising waters could be a problem here in the future. There are no dunes or other rises and no plants to speak of, no sea grass or palm trees, just sand. The palm trees all died in an early 1990s blight. There is just sand, no rocks, just sand. Yes, erosion is a problem, and hurricanes wreak havoc on the beaches here. The area has no hotels or high-rise condos, just one and two story private homes, many painted in bright colors. It is beach as far as one can see with a constant breeze and several shades of turquoise in the waters, changing six or seven times before they disappear over the horizon.

At times, there is only the sea to gaze upon; at times, the air is full of birds following schools of fish and shrimp. And yet other times, there are the bright colors of the sails of the sailboats. Occasionally a yacht will go by and many smaller pleasure crafts dot the landscape. Early in the morning and then again in the evening, the old wooden shrimpers and fishing boats make their way out to sea and back. Early today, before the boats arrived, a dolphin swam slowly by, playfully, effortlessly making his way down the beach.

Is this a nice beach? That is a relevant question. If you are from Indiana and have never swum in warm salt water, this is close to paradise. The beach at Progreso next door is a port of call for cruise ships. There are several that come every week all year round. They arrive in the mornings; the passengers get shuttled down the six kilometer long pier and take up positions in the sand, turn bright red, eat seafood, drink some beer, buy a cheap souvenir, and return to the ship.

If you are Yucateco, however, this is not paradise. It is just the reasonable alternative to being in the city when it is 106 degrees and there is no fresh breeze. (Quickly for the geographically challenged...Yucatán is two things. One, it is a state in the United States of Mexico. Two, it is a peninsula that straddles North and

Central Americas. The peninsula holds two complete countries, Belize and Guatemala, and parts or all of five states in Mexico. Fortunately, the state of Yucatán is located in the peninsula or this could really get confusing. If you add Honduras to the Yucatán Peninsula, you pretty much have defined the ancient world of the Maya.)

Wow, about one hundred seagulls just flew by; must be a kid with bread crumbs down the beach.

OK, now back to our beach discussion. More or less 200 miles east of here is the eastern side of the Yucatán Peninsula, where the waters are no longer the Gulf of Mexico but the beautiful blue waters of El Mar Caribe, the Caribbean. Yes, that very same Caribbean where all the exotic honeymoon and vacation islands are to be found. The Virgin Islands, Aruba, Martinique, Jamaica, etc. form a crescent of islands in the Caribbean. The coast there is referred to as the Maya Riviera, and I can attest that it is paradise and there is absolutely no comparison. The very owners of the beach house I am using close up this house for at least one week and go to the Caribbean. As for me, I am content for now to stay right here at Chelem. My reservations for the Caribbean aren't for another five weeks!

25

Chicxulub

Chicxulub is fortunately much easier to pronounce and spell than Dzibilchaltún, which you have to pass by to get to Chicxulub from my home in Merida. Those aren't Spanish-sounding names, you say, and you are right. They are Maya names and generally they describe something about the place given those names. The famous spring break resort of Can Cun (the correct spelling is two separate words) literally means "snake's nest." Given the contemporary sociology and narcotrafficing in Can Cun, I would say that it was a pretty good call on the part of the ancient Maya. The name of the famous Maya ruins of Chichén Itzá literally means the "mouth of the well of the Itzá" tribe of Maya. There are in fact not one, but at least three large mouths or openings in the ground that give access to large wells 75 to 300 feet below. Dzibilchaltún is a bit more difficult to translate. I have not seen the research, but my primitive level of Maya would indicate that it means place where a carrot grows straight or something close to that.

Chicxulub, on the other hand, deviates from the pattern of identifying something unique about a place and a strict translation would be "jeez, wouldja look at the size of…" They never finished the size of what because (you science majors are way ahead of me here) Chicxulub is the name of the meteor so big that when it hit the very spot I am standing on (I can still pick up a rock and hear echoes of "jeez, wouldja look at the size of….") it threw so much dirt, dust, two thatch houses, and five really obese Maya priests into the air, that sunlight was blocked out for a long enough period of time that all the dinosaurs and prehistoric animals died out. To quote the early Italian explorers that studied this area, "Thatsa prettya biga rocka."

Now, I am standing in the middle of the Chicxulub crater, in fact my home on the other side of Dzibilchaltún is in the crater, as is everything around here. You really can't tell though, because over the, to be precise, six gazillion, three hundred years, four months, and thirteen days since the meteor hit, the crater has been filled in with part of the Gulf of Mexico, sandy beaches, a few small towns like Dzibilchaltún and Chicxulub, a major city of a million people, some restaurants, and a couple of boutique T-shirt shops.

I come to this spot often to escape the heat of the city and walk the beach for exercise. I almost always come to this same spot at the beach: the eastern end of the *malecon* in Progreso. Progreso is a small fishing village on the coast and the shipping port in the Gulf of Mexico for the city of Merida. A *malecon* is a street that runs alongside of a beach, and there are no buildings on the beach side, just one hundred yards of sand. This *malecon* starts at the pier of Progreso on the west end and runs about one kilometer to my spot on the east end. The pier is six kilometers (four miles) long out into the water, and there is a channel dug out for another two kilometers to allow the big ships to come in. (Remember a big ol' rock from outer space came in and flattened this place, even way out in the gulf, and left it very shallow). When there are visitors to the beach, they generally congregate on the pier end of the *malecon*.

I prefer the quieter, less populated end of the *malecon* where there are no little children crying out "He's going to die" and trying to push me back into the water. When I go into the water on my own volition, I usually wander out about one hundred yards or so until the water gets deep enough for me to float around with just my head bobbing about out of the water. In Mexico, schools don't get out until mid-July, so even now at the end of June, I can pretty much have the whole beach to myself in this little fishing village.

Not so today! The place is jumping with activity. A Carnival cruise ship has docked at the pier, and all the passengers that didn't want to take an all-day trip to the ruins of Chichén Itzá or Uxmal got off the boat and were shuttled to the beach. There are pale white *gringos* everywhere! Many of them just got off the shuttle bus, headed down to the beach near the pier, stripped down to their bathing suits, and started soaking up some rays. Some started long walks the length of the *malecon* and back, and some took advantage of the thatch beach umbrellas provided by the restaurants across the street for patrons needing a refreshing beverage. The remaining few discovered the Jet Ski and banana boat options. To serve the *gringos* under the umbrellas, the waiters needed to carry trays filled with beverages across a busy street, up a small ladder over the two-and-a-half-foot sea wall, and through the sand to the tables under the thatch. These guys are good!

There is a brightly painted double-decker bus with music blaring and a loud speaker so the driver can point out all the really interesting places along the *malecon* of one kilometer, two thirds of a mile, the most interesting of which is a house shaped like a wedding cake on "my" end of the *malecon*. The rest of the time the driver fills the *gringos* in on local culture, like the rich people that own the beach houses live way way far away in Merida (30 minutes away) and only come to their beach houses for two months out of the year, leaving them empty the other ten months. We laugh at much of what the drivers tell the tourists.

For every pale-skinned, soon to be pink, and later to be beet red tourist on the beach, there is a small brown-skinned vendor walking up and down the beach, in and out of the restaurants, hawking their wares. The younger male vendors seem to spend more time around the young pale bikini-clad *gringas* than anywhere else. They almost never make it down to my end of the *malecon*. One can buy clothing, jewelry, silver coins, handcrafts, trinkets, hammocks, Panama hats, pirated DVDs and CDs, and unusually shaped *papalotes* (kites), as well as a variety of food products. In addition to the jet skis and inflated banana shaped yellow floats pulled by yesterday's fishing boats, one can also ride on horseback on the beach or go windsurfing. It's wonderful to see the beach so alive, as long as they stay down toward the pier and away from me!

I am about ready to venture out into the gulf waters and take up my position on my favorite sand bar about one hundred or so yards out. I line myself up with the first blue canopy at the restaurant Viña del Mar, since there are no rocks hidden in the water straight out from the first canopy. I look up and there is a boat heading straight at me, not a dangerous situation since the boat just turned out at the end of the pier and is four miles away but still, heading right at me. There is no pier or dock or anything, just an old *gringo* wanting to go out into the water and let his head bob around for a while. In my curiosity, I delay my entry into the water. The boat keeps heading straight for me, never veering. It gets close enough that I can see that it is a pleasure boat also well rigged for fishing…sleeps maybe six below. The boat finally slowed down, actually stopped, and dropped anchor about one hundred yards straight out from the first blue canopy at the Viña del Mar! "Hey! That's my spot, my own personal spot in the Chicxulub crater that I have been coming to for years!" The words never got out of my mouth, as much as I considered going out and asking them to move their *&#%$^#&* boat, but I counted six heads in the boat and there was only one of me. Handy information to have at a time like that. I went out into the warm gulf waters and veered a little myself so as not to infringe on their privacy and to have a little privacy myself. I actually was a little further out in the gulf than the boat was where it was deep enough to be up to my chin and I could float around with just my head bobbing around in the water. From my vantage point about twenty yards away, I could see that the boat was a beautiful Boston Whaler with twin Yamaha 225s. That puppy could scoot! The six heads turned out to be two little boys about ten or eleven, their mom, their dad, and grandmother. The sixth head was a headrest on the driver's seat. So I spent my time with just my head bobbing about in the water; from a distance, it probably looked like I was a float for one of their long fishing poles.

Occasionally a crazy *gringo* on a jet ski would get down to our quiet end, laughing and swaying back and forth, not really keeping a keen eye out for bobbing heads in the waves. During those times I inched a little closer to the boat, being thankful now for the protection it provided me. Occasionally a banana boat would also venture towards me and invariably lose its occupants. One or two people never fell off a banana boat; if one fell, they all fell off. Whenever people fell off a banana boat, the bald bobbing head had a smile on it.

Somewhere in the world, the sun was over the yardarm (I love to talk nautical). It was time to start phase two of my three-hour lunch, the food and beverage part. We (my sweet spouse and I) had come up to Progreso for a good fresh seafood lunch. The owners of our favorite place on the Caribbean have just opened a restaurant on the *malecon*, "Lafitte's." The wait staff had the same gregarious nature and impeccable service that the Caribbean place is famous for, and the food also measured up to the owner's reputation. It also didn't hurt that my particular beverage of choice was fifty percent cheaper here than in a restaurant in the city. Sitting in the front rows of tables, getting full advantage of the warm salt air can adjust your priorities in life! Soon, too soon, our three hours was about up, and it was time to return to Merida for the daily siesta. I do siesta, really well!

We woke from our siesta, checked our watches, and concluded that there was sufficient time to get dressed, drive around to the other end of the city, pay about three dollars for front row seats, and enter Kukulcán Stadium, home to the Leones de Yucatán, our local AAA baseball team. The old fellow taking tickets smiled and said. "This is your first game this season, welcome back." We went up the steps into the stadium, at least I thought we did, one of us got distracted at the T-shirt and jersey booth, the fellow in charge of beverage services smiled and said "This is your first game this season. Where have you been? Are you alone tonight?" Just then my wife appeared from the clothing booth sans any new T-shirts but with a head full of prices for future reference. We took our seats on the front row, about halfway between the dugout and the pitcher's warm up area, and a voice called down "Dos Montejos *correcto*." The beer vendor for that section remembered our favorite brand. Just then the long time centerfielder, Luis "El Rayo"(insert the sound of a thunder clap because he runs like lightning) Arredondo waved and came over for hugs and handshakes and asked how we had been and that he was glad to see us. "El Rayo" once hit me straight on in the heart with an errant throw, and I suspect that he is always glad to see that I am still alive. Our Montejo beers arrived..."Play Ball"!

Gracias a Dios, it is good to have another day at home in the crater of the Chicxulub meteor.

26

My Heart Cries for Yucatán

Often my heart has cried for Yucatán
It missed the depth of the blue Yucatecan sky
It missed the beaches of the Gulf and the Caribbean
It missed the charm of downtown Merida
It missed the beauty of the people, my friends

But now my heart cries for Yucatán after Hurricane Isadore

My heart cries for the people of the villages
Who have lost their homes for sleeping
Who have lost their crops for eating
Who have lost their boats for fishing
Who have lost their families for loving

My heart cries for the parents who cannot care for their children
My heart cries for the children who are hungry
My heart cries for the elderly who are ill
My heart cries for all the ones made homeless
My heart cries for all who wonder how a loving God
could allow this to happen

My heart cries for Yucatán

Alan Van Bodegraven

Translated into Spanish by Blanca Zendejas and printed in the La Voz, *the Spanish language newspaper of Burlington, North Carolina.*

27

Yucagringa

I have been in Yucatán for nineteen years, and I have always had Maya friends. Most of my Maya friends live in pueblos a distance from the capital city of Merida and live very traditional Maya lives. The men make *milpa* (farm) and the women cook, make clothing, hammocks, etc. It is a culture where most people are basically equal and, though like any society it has its problems, in general, they lead very tranquil and happy lives.

Lately I have learned about Maya life in pueblos closer to the city. It is much different than the pueblos that I have previously known. The Maya closer to the city have are often drawn to work in the city where they can make more money than in the village. The result is that they need to adjust to two worlds: the traditional Maya ways of the village, and the ways of a cosmopolitan city and people with money, power, technology, big houses, cars, and education. In this environment, the Maya are clearly second- or third-class citizens. They cannot compete or even hope to compete with the city people. With little education, they are limited to the most menial and humbling of jobs.

I did not understand much about the Maya near the city. Why? Because my experiences were with more remote villages, and I have really only known one Maya from a pueblo nearby: Lucy.

In Spanish we have two words for "to know." One is *saber*, it means to know things. I *saber* the capitals of the states, for example, or I know how congress works. The other word is *conocer*. It means to be familiar with. I *conocer* Chicago, my home, or I *conocer* my children. I *"sabered"* Lucy for eleven years. I knew that she was a nice person that worked hard and that she had a very poor and difficult life. I garnered a lot of respect for her over the years as I saw her work hard and care deeply for her children. But for eleven years, I did not *conocer* Lucy because we did not talk to each other. It wasn't because my Spanish was bad; it was because my Spanish was nearly non-existent. Almost two years ago Lucy came to the house to work and as always asked, "How are you?" I don't remember why, but my reply was, "Sad and lonely." She asked my why I was sad and lonely and we began to talk, slowly, but we were talking...in Spanish of course.

Through time, we began to share many things and feelings and a friendship was developing, but I always felt that there was a distance between us that I was not comfortable or pleased with. I sensed that the distance was due to this society having class levels that we are not accustomed to in the USA. Finally I said to her: "Lucy, if we are to be friends, we need to change a couple of things. One, in my culture we do not have social levels and in my religion, we are all equal. You call me *"patron"* (benevolent owner) and say that you are my *muchacha*. That creates an inequality between us. You use a verb form that is formal with me and expect me to use a verb form that is informal with you. That too creates an inequality between us. So, please, do not call me *patron*, I am Alan, and use only the informal verb form with me. I want to look at you, not down at you." (This is difficult because she is all of 4'10" at the most!) It only took her a day or two and she has never called me *patron* or used the formal verb form again...well, kind of. In public or with her friends, she believes that they cannot accept or understand our cultural violations, and so I am still the *patron* and she the *muchacha*. She is probably right.

Most of the days that Lucy worked, we talked a lot. Sometimes I would help her clean so that we had more time to talk. It was wonderful practice for my Spanish. I learned early on the she needed to laugh to escape the pains and fears of her life. She was very poor, very fearful of what would become of her children, and was in a very bad marriage. So, every time we were together, after the comfortable conversation of "How are the boys, does your husband have work, how is your wife, Alan, one of us would say something totally outrageous, often quite inappropriate. We would laugh, make jokes about the topic at hand, and laugh some more. We have laughed a lot over almost two years. It has been good medicine for both of us. Sometimes life was just too heavy and painful for Lucy, and she needed to cry before she could laugh. I would put my arm around her, and she would put her head on my shoulder to cry. But eventually we would laugh. We always managed to laugh. That is our friendship: we cry, we care and we laugh. We are very happy to be friends.

I know Lucy as a liberated woman, a rarity for her culture. It is also a problem for her as her culture does not accept her as a good person because she is liberated. They treat her badly in her village. But to me, she is like a beautiful tropical bird flying from tree to tree. I know her to have a lot of inner strength. I admire her strength, but the men in her village are intimidated by it. I watch her with her children, I have never seen a mother love and enjoy her children as much as she does. In comparison to my material life, Lucy has nothing, but I have seen her give to others less fortunate than she is. She has a big heart, a heart of gold. When I listen to her, I sense that despite a lack of education, she is one of the most intelligent persons that I know.

She has had a life of pain, hunger, fears, disappointments, and serious mistreatment, but through it all, she does not know how to be angry or feel sorry for herself. I find this amazing. There is a tendency among the Maya to simply accept whatever life gives to them. Lucy takes what life gives to her and makes something good happen for her. Lucy has more goals and plans that the rest of her village combined, but they are not dreams, they are things that Lucy is making come true in her life. She never complains about what she does not have, but is joyful for what she does have and proud of what she has accomplished.

Lucy always wears a smile. She has a lot of friends and it is obvious why. Lucy gives love to all people equally and accepts people for who they are. She genuinely cares about their struggles in life. Some days Lucy and some friends come to my house for a few beers and snacks. It is better for them than going to a bar and being harassed by men. I learned from these visits that Lucy is very different from her friends. When I first mentioned that she was different, she was very resistant and insisted that she was just a simple Maya woman and nothing more. With time and a few unfortunate incidents with friends, she has come to understand that she is different in very positive ways and has come to embrace and enjoy being different. I don't want to go into details, but when it comes to a work ethic, taking responsibility for one's life, and how to treat your fellow humans, she is different from the others that I have met from her village.

Underlying all the tears and laughter that we have shared is a friendship founded on total respect and acceptance. This enables the friendship to be free of tension or pressure that often exists in relationships. We are totally free, verbally, with each other, and we can and do share very intimate parts of our hearts and minds with each other. We know that we will not be judged. I have heard her say that we probably have more love between us than most married couples, but our love is as very close friends. We have a very unique friendship.

The growth in our friendship this year was, in part, due to some sad events. In the space of about a month, her fifteen-year-old son left home to make his way in the world as an assistant to a manual laborer, her shiftless, ne'er-do-well husband (it's my book, I can editorialize) bailed out on her, and she discovered a lump in her breast. We had some tears together that particular month. We had some hugs, and yes, we still found things to laugh about. She is a very strong woman, but always gentle and caring. She knows that in reality, we are not equals, but that I look up to her.

We are very much alike, Lucy and me. Our countenance is the same, we think alike, our sense of humor is the same, and we share many of the same values. We enjoy learning from and teaching each other. For a long time, she did not believe that I could love her, but that too changed.

Lucy's friends tell her, "Lucy, you are lucky to have Alam at your side." (The Maya cannot close a word with an "n", they pronounce my name as Alam) I told Lucy, "I like that they understand that I am at your side and not just your patron, but there is

Lucy 2008

something very flawed about their comments. Lucy, my friend, there is no such thing as luck. Your friends sit around and complain about their lives and wait for luck to jump on them like luck was a rabbit just jumping from person to person without rhyme or reason, or luck is God or a government giving to some persons and not others things that they didn't have to work for. But you, Lucy, you cleaned my toilet for thirteen years, you washed my underwear for thirteen years, and you never complained or asked for anything but an opportunity to work and put food on the table for your children. You work hard, you are honest, and I have always been able to have total trust and confidence in you. Thirteen years of hard work is not luck. Don't you think that maybe you have earned some respect and some friendship? Everything that you have ever received from my wife and me you earned and deserved. Your friends see our 'gifts' to you, but they are nothing more than your *alguinaldo* (year-end bonus) being delivered in pieces. You are not lucky, you are worthy." I held her hands as I talked. She cried. I cried.

Later that night I received a message on my cell phone from Lucy. "Alan, I am sitting alone in the town square of my village thinking about our conversation. I now understand that you do not love me as a woman, but as a person."

Lucy is without doubt Maya of Yucatán. However in many ways she is very much like this old *gringo*. That is why, to me, she is a yucagringa. If this yucagranga and I were lovers or spouses, I could not love her more than I do now as a friend.

Alan & Lucia Socorro Yah Miam – May 2008

Preface
Nojoch K'ai, Ozzie and Me

I wrote this by request, sort of. In an elementary school in rural Pennsylvania, there was an eight year old boy of color in a second grade class. He was the only person of color in the class and one of only two in the whole school.

The class had a project to engage the students in learning about geography and cultures. They each had a cardboard doll named Stanley—actually, because of the shape of the cardboard, "Flat Stanley." They painted clothing and faces on the dolls. The object was to take the Flat Stanleys to their homes and send them on vacations with family, neighbors, and friends. They were to take photos and collect brochures to bring back. The children were to share the adventures of their Flat Stanley with the class as a lesson on geography and culture.

The teacher was concerned that the little boy of color would not be successful in this endeavor because his family and social circles did not have the means to travel or have interest in his education. He needed some help. The teacher called me and asked if I could take the little boy's Flat Stanley to Yucatán with me. I agreed to do it and decided that this Flat Stanley should keep a journal.

So, I wrote a journal as Flat Stanley, on his 4,000-mile trip to Yucatán, his three months in Yucatán, and his encounters with the indigenous Maya of Yucatán and Chiapas. We arrived in Yucatán in November, and I sent Flat Stanley back to Pennsylvania at the end of January. The journal is designed to be read to eight- and nine-year-old children. I enjoyed writing it for children. I hope that you enjoy reading it.

I called the teacher later on and asked how the journal went over with the children. It received rave reviews, and the teacher said, "Thanks, Dad".

Nojoch K'ai, Ozzie and Me

Written by Flat Stanley for his friend Zyon

Flat Stanley, Njjoch K'ai, and Ozzie

I Flat Stanley, strongly suggest that you read this story with maps of the United States and of Mexico at your side so that you can follow our adventure.

Nojoch K'ai, Ozzie, and I, Flat Stanley, are going to travel from North Carolina in the United States to Merida, Yucatán in Mexico. Our journey will be about 4,000 miles going through seven states in the United States of America and six states in the United States of Mexico. I will spend two months in Yucatán learning about the Maya of thousands of years ago and the Maya of today. Many people call the Maya "Indians," but Nojoch K'ai says that Indians are from India and that the Maya are the . . . get ready for a new big word . . . indigenous people of the Yucatán. Indigenous means people who were the first people there. In the United States we have indigenous people like the Cherokee, Navajo, Seminoles, all of the "Indians" that were here when Columbus arrived, but we won't use the word Indian anymore. The Maya, about two thousand years ago, the same time as all the Bible stories happened, were the most sophisticated and intelligent people on the earth. While the Romans were good soldiers, the Maya were good mathematicians, astronomers, and engineers. I am looking forward to meeting them.

Ozzie

Nojoch K'ai lives in Yucatán, and we are going to his home there. Nojoch K'ai is Maya for "You're the man" or" You da man." Many of the Maya call him Nojoch K'ai. Nojoch K'ai is pronounced "No hoe ch kah eye." Ozzie is Nojoch K'ai's six-month-old black kitten. In Maya, Ozzie is a *box mis* (bowsh meese), a black cat. I hope for us that he is a good luck black cat.

Tuesday, November 13, 2007

It is seven o'clock in the morning, and we are starting our adventure. We are leaving from Burlington, North Carolina. North Carolina is one of the thirteen original colonies that signed the Declaration of Independence to become the first states in the United States. Although its name is "North" Carolina, it is in the south of the United States between Virginia and South Carolina. The east side of North Carolina is on the Atlantic coast. The west side is part of the Appalachian Mountains. Burlington is in the middle, in the piedmont. In the piedmont, there have been tobacco farms, furniture factories, and knitting mills where they would take cotton grown in the south and make fabric and knit clothing. The water in the rivers flowing from the mountains to the coast could generate electricity to run the machines in the factories. The workers, especially in the knitting mills, were treated badly by the company owners and had very bad working conditions. One day a very common and ordinary woman named Norma Rae, decided that things had to change, and so she stood up to the owners and demanded that the workers be allowed to form a union to get better working conditions. You can rent the movie and see it for yourselves, but after a long hard struggle, the unions came, and the lives of the workers were better. She did not have an education, political power, or riches; she only had a vision of what was right and the courage to try to make it happen.

The first city that we drove through was Greensboro, North Carolina. Something very important happened here many years ago. In our country in the south, there were a lot of tobacco and cotton farms, or as they called the cotton farms, plantations. The problem was that they did not have enough people to work the fields, so that brought Africans here to work in the fields. Unfortunately, the Africans were not treated as people, but as property. Well, eventually there was a war between the northern states and the southern states called the Civil War. One of the results of the war was that the African workers were now free. Well, they were free, but they did not have equality with other Americans. Almost 100 years later some college students of color, not rich or powerful people, just some college students of color, went into a restaurant and asked to be served. The restaurant refused to serve people of color, so the college students refused to leave the restaurant. This action along with an action of an older woman in Alabama showed the world that not all Americans had equal rights and that it was time to change. Again, a case of ordinary people with a vision of what is right, and some courage, changing the world. Today, people of all colors in the United States are equal.

We drove through North Carolina, through South Carolina and Georgia into Alabama and drove half way through Alabama. South Carolina ands Georgia have a lot of peanut and peach farms. The town of Gaffney, South Carolina, has the city water tower painted up to look like a giant peach. We drove through the big city of Atlanta, Georgia. Halfway through Alabama we stopped in the city of Montgomery for our first night. Montgomery, Alabama, is where an older woman, Rosa Parks, tired after a long days work, refused to go to the back of the bus where all the African Americans were supposed to sit. She figured that she had a right to sit anywhere she wanted. It was this older woman, like the college students in North Carolina, who had a vision of what was right and the courage to stand up for it. These ordinary people did extraordinary things. This part of Alabama was also where a great African-American preacher started to send out the message of equality for all. He was, of course, the great Martin Luther King.

We started the second day by driving the rest of the way through Alabama and through Mississippi and Louisiana. We stopped right as we left Louisiana and got into Texas. The states had lots of old cotton plantations and different kinds of farms. We took a little detour and drove down into New Orleans. Remember that a year or so ago, Hurricane Katrina hit and flooded New Orleans? We were curious if we could see damage and recovery from the highway. Well, it was all there to see without leaving the interstate. Well, there was neighborhood after neighborhood where the houses were damaged beyond repair. There were many other neighborhoods where there was a white trailer in almost all front yards where the family was living while their homes were being repaired. It was painful to see all the destruction.

When we entered Texas it was at the mileage marker 877. This road went 877 miles through Texas! We are driving about 550 miles each day. We could never drive through Texas in one day! Driving through Texas would be like driving from Philadelphia, Pennsylvania, to Pittsburgh, Pennsylvania, three times!

Our third day was going to be a short day, only about 350 miles, so we planned to leave a little later than normal. We left later even though Ozzie woke us all up at 4:30 in the morning with wet kisses on the nose, loud purring, and tapping our heads with his paws. With Ozzie around, we never needed to set an alarm clock because Ozzie always woke us up early. Speaking of Ozzie, he, like I said, is only six months old and this is his first trip and he is not doing very well. Cats are normally very sure-footed and nimble but that is not possible when the floor is moving as the car rolls along! Physically, it is very frightening for him to have his floor moving and swaying back and forth. He hates it and has been crying himself hoarse for two days. His voice now sounds like a ninety-six-year-old cat!

San Antonio was our second stop in Texas. It is a very famous and unique city. Its architecture, food, and many of the people are very similar to old Mexico in style. The reason is that this part of Texas used to be part of Mexico. Over the years, the United States gained possession of this area. It is the heart of the famous Texas cattle ranches and the famous cowboy times in our history. Another unique thing about San Antonio is that where the San Antonio River winds around the city, there is a whole other city below street level along the banks of the river. They call it The Riverwalk, and it is filled with wonderful restaurants and shops. You can take a boat cruise, even a dinner cruise along the river, and hear live Mexican music being played from place to place. It is a little strange to sit in a boat and look up at a street!

San Antonio is also famous for having several old Spanish missions around the town. When the Spanish came to this part of the world, they brought Catholic priests with them. When they would conquer a village, a small church or mission was built to try to get the indigenous people there to be Catholics. The missions around San Antonio are very pretty. The city is also known for the Alamo. The Alamo was an old Spanish fort built hundreds of years ago near the San Antonio River. Remember when I said that this used to be part of Mexico? Well, a bunch of Americans took over the Alamo, and this upset the Mexicans very much. So, General Santa Ana and a big army of Mexicans came up to get the Alamo back. There were only a handful of Americans to defend the Alamo against a huge army. The Americans knew that they did not have a chance, but decided to fight to the very end, to die if necessary. The battle, which should have taken a few hours, took several days. Eventually Santa Ana and his army won the battle and all the Americans died. When the word got out about how bravely the Americans fought, the battle at the Alamo became a symbol of courage. Whenever people needed to be encouraged, someone would cry out, "Remember the Alamo."

The Alamo is still there in San Antonio and thousands of people visit it every day.

Nojoch K'ai had meetings for two days, so Ozzie and I just relaxed at the hotel. On Sunday we started out in the car again, driving to the Mexican-American border. We spent the night in Brownsville, Texas, which is about as far south as possible to be and still be in the United States. When we first entered Texas a few days ago, it was oil country. There were oil wells and huge refineries that took the oil and made gas to heat your homes, gas to run your cars, and a lot of other products that can be made from oil. Like I said before, we were now in old cowboy country. On the drive from San Antonio to the border we went past HUGE ranches and farms. We went through one ranch that was so big . . . (you are supposed to ask, "How big was it?"), well, let me put it to you this way. Small things are measured in inches. Bigger things are measured in feet or yards. Even bigger things are measured in acres or miles. The King Ranch in Texas is so big that it is measured in Rhode Islands. That's right, the state of Rhode Island. The King Ranch in Texas is five times bigger than the state of Rhode Island! That's a lot of cows!

Did you know that Americans were not the first cowboys? When the Spanish came over, they settled more in Mexico and in Central and South America. They moved north up into Texas and California later. When they came, along with the catholic priests, they brought soldiers, cattle, and horses. They taught the Mexicans how to rope and ride and later the Mexicans taught these skills to the Americans. Even the word "rodeo" is a Spanish word.

As usual Ozzie woke everybody up early on border crossing day. We crossed into Mexico at 6:00 in the morning. Nojoch K'ai is a legal resident of Mexico, so we did not need to go through immigration. We did, however, need to go through customs and get permission to bring a vehicle into Mexico. All of that took about thirty minutes, and then we were then driving through the sleepy morning streets of Matamoros, in the state of Tamaulipas in Mexico. When we left Matamoros, we drove for nearly eight hours without seeing another city. We passed through some small villages, but nothing large enough to need a stoplight. The

Northern Mexico in Tamaulipas

land we saw in the morning was totally flat and used for farming. It looked a little like the flat lands of Kansas. In the afternoon, the flat lands gave way to gentle rolling hills of lush green and valleys with big cattle ranches. In the distance we could see some mountain tops.

We went straight south for a couple of hours and then took another road that went southeast, aimed at the coast of the Gulf of Mexico. We eventually did get to another city, Tampico. We went

Tuxpan

around the outside of Tampico and did not go into town. Tampico is on the coast and has a lot of big commercial ships in the harbor. However, because we bypassed the city, still have not seen the coast. After Tampico, we drove a couple of hours and stopped in the pretty little town of Tuxpan.

It is pronounced "Toosh pahn." The town is where a river comes from inland and joins the Gulf of Mexico. The town is built along the river and has great seafood restaurants.

I should probably tell you that Ozzie and I do not have a clue what is going on around us. All of the signs, billboards, and everything are in Spanish. The people we meet at gas stations and restaurants speak only Spanish. The road signs to tell you how far away the next town is or how fast you can drive are in kilometers instead of miles. We were on a road where you could drive 100 kilometers an hour, but that is not very fast. You need to know how to do algebra math to figure out that 100 kilometers an hour is about 65 miles an hour. Also, there are no McDonalds or KFCs around here. You can eat gorditas or tamales or empanadas or camarones, but no hamburgers and fries. Even the money

Mexican Pesos

"Dad, did you remember to put the horse in the truck? He wanted to go to town."

"Dad, did you remember to put the pigs in the truck? They wanted to go to the mall with us."

You only have to buckle your seatbelt if you have a seatbelt

is different. You cannot use dollars here, only pesos. What is unusual about the Mexican money is that unlike American paper money that is all green and the same size, the paper pesos are different colors and sizes. When we buy gasoline in the United States it is about three dollars a gallon. Here we are paying seven pesos a liter. Is that good or bad? Nojoch K'ai says that seven pesos a liter is about $2.50 dollars a gallon; that is good. I can't figure out how he does that.

A word about Ozzie, since I tattled on him earlier. Yesterday and today he was a perfect traveler. Oh, he still lets us know that he doesn't like being in the mini-van, but every morning he jumps into his travel bag and is ready to go for another ride. Actually he doesn't mind the mini-van, but he doesn't like for whatever he is standing on to move. It takes away his confidence. Yesterday and today he would complain a little and then go up to Nojoch K'ai, give him a kiss, and then settle down on a big box and watch traffic and sleep. Okay, this is my new Spanish word for the day: *bache*, "bah chay". It means pothole. Most of today

Of course, not everyone drives a truck.

The bus that slid off the road

there were thousands of baches in the roads. Earlier in our travels if the car hit a little bump, Ozzie would complain for thirty minutes. Today whenever we hit a bache, Ozzie would just look up and then go back to sleep or watching traffic.

I should tell you that one frightening thing happened. At one of the many road construction sites there was no pavement, only a dirt road with some rain, which made it a muddy slippery road, like driving on ice. People here don't have any experience with driving on something as slippery as ice. A big passenger bus in front of us lost control and slid off the road. Fortunately, no one was hurt. The lesson is that if a professional bus driver can slide off the road, the rest of us better be very careful.

Day eight of our trip to Yucatán

Yesterday was Monday; tomorrow will be Wednesday, so today must be Tollday. Today we reached our third state in Mexico. First we entered Mexico in Tamaulipas, and then stayed the first night in Tuxpan in the state of Veracruz. Today, Tollday, we drove twelve hours, 527 miles and entered the state of Chiapas. Normally we would not go through Chiapas but here is the reason that we did today.

Earlier today we drove into the isthmus of Mexico. That's a funny word, isthmus. It sounds like when someone tries to say Christmas with three front teeth missing . . . "Crith mus."

The prairie, a lake with egrets and the mountains in the west

Crithmus, isthmus . . . whatever. An isthmus is a place where a land becomes very narrow and then opens up into a bigger land again. The isthmus in Mexico has two states in it: Tabasco on the north side along the Gulf of Mexico and Chiapas to the south with mountains and the Pacific Ocean coast. Not long ago there were very heavy rainfalls in the isthmus, and the state of Tabasco ended up 80 percent flooded, and we could not drive through it. Instead we had to drive south up into the mountains and go around the state of Tabasco. Basically we had to drive south and east until we almost reached the country of Guatemala in Central America and turn left! The mountains were not flooded, although we did have to keep an eye out for land and mud slides coming down off of the mountains. After crossing a spectacularly beautiful lake going from the state of Veracruz into Chiapas, we stopped for the night in the city of Tuxla Gutierez. Oh, why did I call today "Tollday"? Today we had to pay tolls twelve different times. We spent more than $75 in tolls! I think that the people in the state of Veracruz need to pay a toll to back out of their driveway! We think that if we pay a toll, the toll road will be a better road. Well, some of them were, but others were narrow, windy, and full of *baches* (potholes). If those were the good roads, I can't imagine how bad the free roads are!

The early hours today took us to the port city of Veracruz in the state of Veracruz. As we got close to Veracruz, the city, we got our first view of the coast of the Gulf of Mexico even though we had been near the coast for a hundred miles or more. The water was green in color and the area is called the "Emerald Coast." It goes for about thirty miles. As we neared the end of the Emerald Coast, it became very scenic with pretty beaches and palm trees on one side of the car and a good view of the Sierra Madre mountains on the other. On the other side of the Sierra Madre mountains is the capital of Mexico, Mexico City, or as they call it here, "DF." "DF" means district federal. Did you know that Mexico City has twenty-four million people? I cannot imagine twenty-four million of anything, especially twenty-four million people. If the valley is full of twenty-four million people, there is no room to grow food, and it must come in over the mountains every day. How many trucks, do you suppose, it takes to bring fruits, vegetables, meats, and macaroni and cheese for twenty-four million people? I can't begin to imagine the answer. Mexico City has a problem because it was built on top of an old lake bed. That is not a good foundation for a city, and over the years the weight of the city has been making it sink into the ground. To enter the main cathedral downtown, for example, you need to walk down several steps to get to the first floor! Here is another interesting fact about Mexico City. When I think of snow or ice-capped mountains, I think of places like Wyoming, a place with long hard winters. I would never guess that you could find ice-capped mountains way south in the tropics. Well, right outside of Mexico City there are two mountains that are so tall and so cold at the top, there is an ice cap on them all year around. Not only that, they are also active volcanoes! If you flew into Mexico City airport, you could see the smoke of the volcanoes. Ready for two new words? The names of the volcanoes are not Spanish words but Nauatl, the language of the Aztecs who lived in the valley before the Spanish came over. The names are Iztaccihuatl and Popocatepetl! OK, let's try that again . . . "Iz-tock-sea-waddle" and" Poe-Poe-ca-tep-ittle".

In addition to it being Tollday, it was a very green day. The state of Veracruz is very green with beautiful lush green farms, banana plantations, and citrus orchards. When we left Veracruz

A banana plantation in Veracruz

to enter into Chiapas, we also entered very lush, tropical mountains and valleys. Chiapas is truly one of the most beautiful places that I have been. Tomorrow we will drive across the mountain tops, turn north, and head for the Yucatán Peninsula. Tonight we will spend the night in Tuxla Gutierez, and we could not find a hotel that would let us take Ozzie inside, so he has to

A mountain top lake as we entered Chiapas

spend the night in the car. We hope that he will be alright.

How did Ozzie do in the mini-van last night? He did just fine, but he was very angry about it. Normally whenever a door or window would open, he would just look and meow. He was always a little afraid of what might be outside; remember, he is only six months old. Today was different. He was so angry he howled at everything all morning ,and whenever we had to open a door or window to pay for gas or ANOTHER toll, he would leap toward the opening to try to escape from the mini-van. He had no fear, only anger. Every time Nojoch K'ai caught Ozzie in the nick of time before he flew out of the mini-van. As much as his behavior was a problem, there is a good side to it.

In this part of Mexico, there is a lot of drug trafficking and illegal immigrants from Central America, so there are a lot of places where the army has set up checkpoints. At the checkpoints, everyone has to get out of the car, and the soldiers look at all of the stuff in your vehicle for drugs or other illegal things. Oh, can you see the problem coming? Ozzie is going to escape when we all have to get out of the car. Now, we didn't have any drugs or other illegal things in the mini-van, but we did have some unusual things that tourists don't normally have with them. We start of course with an eight-month supply of kitty litter and kitten food. In Mexico, cats live outdoors and eat mice; they don't use kitty litter in a box! We also had a large box that contained cat furniture! Next to that box was a box that has an inflatable Christmas decoration . . . a six foot tall Santa Claus in a bathing suit, laying in a hammock tied to two palm trees. We also had twenty-four coffee cups in two of the many boxes in the car. We will have to explain all of this stuff while Ozzie is trying to get away. When we drove up to a checkpoint, Nojoch K'ai showed the soldiers his legal residency, that he was not a tourist, but had a legal right to be in Mexico. He then showed the soldiers a list of everything in the mini-van and explained that an angry cat was about to leap into their faces trying to escape. Just about then, right on cue, Ozzie would howl and leap toward to opening in the window. The startled soldiers would quickly give Nojoch K'ai the list back and wave us through the checkpoint. We never once had to get out of the mini-van and have our stuff inspected by the solders. Good for Ozzie!

We left Tuxla Gutierez early in the morning. It is a surprisingly busy city in the middle of sleepy mountain villages. This area of Mexico has an interesting history. One, the indigenous people here are the Tzotzil branch of the Maya. There are twenty-five different types of Maya peoples and languages. In Mexico, there are more than fifty different types of indigenous peoples. Some of the names you may have heard: Aztecs, Mixtecs, Toltecs, Olmecs, and the Maya. We will be having our explorations with the Yucatec Maya and the Tzotzil Maya. There is so much to see and experience here, but we will not stop and do anything for two reasons. One is that this is day 9 of traveling, and we are tired and want to get home to Yucatán. Two, we will be coming back here in January with college students to learn about everything. Oh, back to the interesting history about this area. Despite the land being lush and fertile, because of many social injustices, the people here are very poor. Also, there are many illegal immigrants of Tzotzil Maya from the country of Guatemala where there was much oppression of the Maya. This made even more poor people in the streets begging. About 1993, many tourists and tourist busses going through this area were stopped by bandits and robbed. It became a dangerous place to be. The bandits were not really bandits, but the poor farmers and unemployed people, organized by a man in a mask called sub-comomdante Marcos. They were using the stolen money to buy guns and bullets. On January 1, 1994, they staged an armed uprising against the Mexican government and Mexican army. Marcos was an educated man, and he used the internet to inform the world of how terrible the conditions were here. The world then kept a close eye on the Mexican government and army to see if they would abuse the poor people even more. The struggle lasted a long time, and eventually some gains were made by the poor people. They called themselves "Zapatistas" after Emilio Zapata, one of the leaders of the Mexican Revolution almost 100 years ago. So, this part of Mexico would be our drive for the first part of today!

The drive early today was long and difficult. Normally we would get on the road and go fifty or sixty miles an hour all day. In the mountains, our speed ranged between almost nothing and thirty-five miles an hour. It was almost nothing when we would get caught behind a double-trailer truck trying to go up a mountain, and then when we could pass them, we got up to about thirty-five miles an hour before we had to slow down for another sharp curve around the mountain. The roads were very narrow, sometimes not even two lanes when part of the road had fallen off the mountain or was covered by a landslide. Ozzie did not help with his constant howling and jumping on Nojoch K'ai's face! Ozzie hated the constant swerving of the mini-van as it went back and forth around the mountain turns. It took us five hours to get across and down the mountains. It was tiresome; it was tedious; and it was hard and long. It was also equally beautiful. I thought that the day before had spectacular views; today was even more spectacular. At one point, we were up high enough that we looked down at the clouds in a valley and a wonderful sunrise over the clouds. The mountains and valleys were a collection of different brilliant shades of green. There were beautiful mountain lakes and quaint villages. There were rows of corn and orange trees climbing straight up a mountainside. All of it was very breathtaking! The farms had to be all worked by hand, since there was no way you could operate a tractor or other equipment on the steep hills. I looked at it and thought that I would probably fall down the mountain.

Can you imagine me in the emergency room at the hospital with two broken legs and a face all beat up? The doctor would come in and ask, "How did you get both of your legs broken and your face all beat up with what looks like the marks that an ear of corn might make?" "Well, Doc," I would say. "I sneezed, lost my balance, and fell off my farm." "You did what?" he would ask. "I fell off my farm," I would tell him. But I would be able to tell that he didn't believe me.

A roadside fruit stand in Chiapas

Food, clothing, you can buy anything on the side of the road

We came down out of the mountains near the ruins of the ancient city of Palenque. We bought some more gas and started the second part of our day. (Have you noticed that I have never mentioned stopping and eating? That is because we never did stop and eat; we just drove all day every day.) We entered the state of Campeche ("Kom-pay-chay"). Campeche and Yucatán have the best roads in all of Mexico, so we would travel twice as far in the afternoon than we did in the morning. It was

Looking down into a Maya village in Chiapas

Early morning in Chiapas looking down on the clouds in the valley

Sunrise in the mountains

also very flat which helped a lot.

About 2:00 in the afternoon, we saw a welcome sight: a white beach, beautiful palm trees, and deep blue waters of the Gulf of Mexico. If you look at a map or two, you can see what we have just done. In North Carolina, the Gulf of Mexico was southwest of us. In Alabama through Louisiana, it was south of us. Down through Texas, Tamaulipas, and Veracruz, it is was east of us. We drove through the mountains, and now the Gulf of Mexico is north of us. We have driven nearly all the way around the Gulf of Mexico!

It was just getting dark when we pulled in front of our Yucatán home. We had left Tuxla Gutierez a little less than twelve hours ago, and we were exhausted. We would spend the next few days unloading our stuff, putting everything away, and putting our feet up to relax. Silly Ozzie! The next morning he voluntarily climbed back into his travel bag; he was ready for another day in the mini-van, he did not know that this was his new home!

The Gulf of Mexico at Sabancoy

"I'm not spending one more day in the car!"

Nojoch K'ai's home in Yucatán

Things that the Maya use in their daily lives (and Ozzie underneath)

My first Maya friend, Lucia de Socorro Yah Miam

A Mexican wedding

Saturday, November 24, we went to a Mexican wedding. In Mexico you don't just go to a wedding and make plans to do something later. In Mexico, you go to a wedding all day and into the night. It starts out in mid-morning with a Catholic mass. The first difference that you notice from weddings in the United States is that it is more family oriented. In the United States, there are usually four or five bridesmaids and an equal number of groomsmen. In Mexico, every little brother and sister, cousin, niece, nephew, etc., is part of the wedding. In this wedding, all of the children from both families were dressed in matching orange dresses or orange shirts with khaki shorts. Even little babies were dressed in orange. Every child old enough to walk was part of the procession.

After the mass, we all went outside of the city where the reception was being held in a Maya village that was built around an old hacienda, an old plantation. In Yucatán, the plantations didn't grow cotton like they did in the United States, they grew henequen. Henequen is a plant that looks like a small cactus.

Children with the bride at the old hacienda

Inside the plant are fibers with a zillion little barbs on them, like little fish hooks, so that when you rub two fibers of henequen together, they grab onto each other. You can make strings of henequen as thick or as long as you want because it all clings together naturally. Oh, you know what henequen is; you call it rope!

OK, back to the wedding reception. The hacienda, named San Diego Tixcacab ("Teesh-cah-cahb") was in beautiful condition, of Spanish style, and painted a deep red. The reception was under several big white tents, and there were big round tables for ten people each with white tablecloths, very fancy dishes, and plants for decorations. There were chairs for probably three hundred guests. There was a live band and all the traditional dancing. People all didn't come at one time, people were arriving all afternoon. The dancing and eating went on all day and into the night.

I should mention the food. We ate something very common in Yucatán, *panuchos*, ("pa-new-chose"). Have you ever eaten a *panucho*? Here is how to make one. The next time your mother is making corn tortillas . . . your mother does make her own corn tortillas, doesn't she? . . . just as she takes the tortilla off the *comal*. Oh, your mother uses a stove. Okay, when she takes the tortilla off of the stove, she needs to blow into it and make it like a little pocket. That can set around all day. When it is time to make the *panuchos*, spread some refried beans inside of the tortilla and then deep fry it so it will be stiff enough to put things on top of it. When it is fried stiff, put some shredded turkey, a tomato slice, some onion, and some guacamole or an avocado slice on top. And now, you have yourself a *panucho*!

Did you know that couples in Mexico need to get married twice...no, not because of divorces or anything. It is because the government doesn't believe that a church wedding is legal, so they need to have a civil ceremony for a legal wedding by somebody like a judge or a justice of the peace. Then, the church doesn't believe that a civil wedding is good without the blessings of the church, so they need to have a church wedding, too. You only have to serve cake and ice cream at one of them!

A Mexican Christmas

Christmas in Yucatán is pretty much the same as it is in the Pennsylvania, except that there is no snow. It was 85 degrees on Christmas day. The neighbors thought that the Santa in a hammock was pretty funny. I don't know how Santa comes in Mexico; there are no chimneys because there are no fireplaces in the tropics.

We spent Christmas Eve with the Erosa family. Dr. Arturo Erosa Barbachano is about 85 years old. He has three daughters and a son. They have about ten grandchildren. So there were

Santa in his hammock and bathing suit!

about twenty-five people for Christmas dinner. The family gathers at someone's house about ten o'clock at night, have a few drinks, and talk a lot. Close to midnight they start the *posada*—to act the part of Mary and Joseph searching for a place to stay in Bethlehem. One half of the family stays inside the house while the other half goes outside. The outside group sings a song asking to be let in for the night. The inside group sings back that there is no room. They move from door to door. If a neighborhood sings the *posada*, they go from house to house. Finally, after singing about five times and very poorly I might add, the people inside welcome them in. A few bible verses are read, and then Nojoch K'ai and his wife Donna sing a Christmas carol, very nicely, I think. After that, everyone sits down to a huge meal. There is turkey, chicken, ham, roast beef, all kinds of casseroles, and vegetables, and, of course, sweet desserts. It's great!

On Christmas day we went to the Torres family. Dr. Helbert and Nellie Torres are in their seventies and have eight children and twenty-six grandchildren. You need a pretty big house to have all these people there. Usually with the family and guests like us, there are about fifty people for dinner. We had a few drinks, talked for a while, then sat down to another huge dinner like the night before! One of the Torres' sons, Juan Carlos, lets Nojoch K'ai use his beach house on the Gulf of Mexico whenever he wants to. Pretty nice friends! That is really neat when it is 110 degrees in Yucatán.

Today is December 31st, New Year's Eve. We are going to be with the Erosa family again tonight. Again, we will gather about ten o'clock in the evening for a few drinks and chatting. Now let's talk about how a Yucatecan New Years works.

First, Nojoch K'ai brought down enough little gifts, some useful, some funny, for everybody to receive one. The host of the party took the gifts and put each one in a small bag along with some candies. When you go to the party you need to take some new red underwear and give it to the host, who then puts the red underwear in each of the gift bags. She numbers the bags and then put the same numbers, each one in a balloon.

Just before midnight someone reads something inspirational. Right at midnight everyone yells "Happy New Year" and runs around kissing and hugging each other. Sounds pretty normal so far . . . except for the underwear thing. After hugging and kissing everybody, you drink some champagne and eat twelve grapes representing the next twelve months of the new year. If you want to travel in the next twelve months, you needed to bring a suitcase and walk around the block with it. You then pick up a small plastic bag and go over to a table with grains on it. Pick up some kernels of corn that represents family, some wheat that represents work, some rice that represents wealth, some birdseed for joy, and some lentils for happiness. You need to carry this bag with you all through the year and all those things will go well for you.

Then you go over to the balloons, pick one, and pop it to get the piece of paper with the number on it. When you get the number, you get the gift bag with the same number and someone's red underwear in it. You need to wear someone else's red underwear, on your sleeve, on your head like a hat, however you please, until you find the real owner and give it back to them. Finally, someone had built an old man of paper and straw and old clothes. You set the old man on fire to symbolize that the old year is now gone. Nojoch K'ai says that he tries to not stand still very long on New

Year's Eve for fear that someone might try to set him on fire!

Now that the new year has started, we will start hanging around with the college students and learning about the Maya. On January fourth, we went to the Museum of Anthropology in Merida. It is a huge beautiful building that used to be a mansion of one of the plantation owners. We couldn't take photos, but I can tell you that it has a lot of artifacts recovered from the various ancient Maya cities. The most interesting thing I learned was that the Maya have two calendars: a civil calendar (a calendar of days and months) and another calendar of religious dates. The calendars have a different numbers of months and days in the months so one is larger than the other. They are like two wheels with cogs that rotate in opposite directions so one can see what civil and religious day

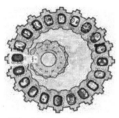

The Maya Calendars

it is. The civil calendar (*haab*) has eighteen months of twenty days, and the religious one (*Tzolkin*) has thirteen months of twenty days. The first civil day of the year and the first religious day of the year are on the same day once every fifty-two years!

The first ancient Maya cities that we will visit are about two thousand or more years old. The first one we visited was Dzibilchaltun ("dzee-beel-chall-toon"). Like other Maya cities, it was located where two essential elements for life could be found: water and land with enough dirt to grow food. There was always a problem finding water in the northern part of Yucatán because of something very interesting. One gazillion, or maybe two gazillion, years ago, a huge meteor fell from the sky and landed right here in Yucatán. The impact threw so much dirt and dust into the air, it blocked out sunlight for a long time so long that plants that the animals ate died. and so did the animals . . . and that was the end of the dinosaurs! The name of the meteor is Chicxulub ("cheek-chew-lube"). The meteor smashed the dirt and rocks and made them very porous, so they can't hold up water for a lake or a river. All the rain went down into the earth and created underground lakes and rivers. Sometimes the earth would wear away,

The Temple of the Dolls at Dzibilchaltun

The Dzibilchaltun Cenote

and the Maya could have access to the water below. Then they could build a city there.

Dzibilchaltun is known for two specific parts of the ancient city. One is a temple named The Temple of Seven Dolls. The temple has an opening that goes all the way through it that is lined up with the stars so that every March 21, the equinox, the sun rises right in the opening, and it looks like the sun is coming from the opening. The second thing is the underground water supply is very close to the ground and it is a great place to go swimming. The underground water supplies are called *cenotes* ("say-note-tays"). Dzibilchaltun was never a large city, but it was important in the ancient Maya trade routes. It has been lived in for two thousand years. (In comparison, the United States of America is only 200 years old).

The next day we went to two small villages out in the jungle where many of the Maya people live today. (Now when I say jungle, a lot of people think about the jungles of Africa with gigantic trees and lush green landscapes. This jungle is quite different. Because there is very little topsoil or dirt for the plants to grow in, this jungle is very short. It is still thick, and you would need a machete to cut your way through it; it is just a lot shorter than the African jungle.) The Maya are generally farmers and are very skilled in many things. They grow their own food, build their own houses, make their own clothes, and can do the work of butchers, plumbers, electricians, contractors, architects, everything. They are quite remarkable! The villages we visited were

Tinum and Loop Xul. Tinum has about 5,000 people, schools, medical clinics, and even a few cars. It is the government center for several smaller towns around it. Loop Xul is further out in the jungle and doesn't have running drinkable water or, until just recently, electricity like the larger towns have. Many of the people in Tinum have specific skills like being a carpenter or a butcher or a maker of cakes for weddings. In Loop Xul, we visited a family that in addition to farming the land, make money by going out into the jungle and pulling vines off of the trees. They

This is a na, *a Maya hut*

My friend Lisa reading to Lisita Poot Canul, 12 years old

Schulze eats with Chava while her mother Doña Piedad makes tortillas

boil the vines to soften the skin or bark of the vines and then strip the skin off. They sell the baskets they make, weaving the skinless vines using both their hands and their feet! I have never seen people work so hard.

I think that some photos will tell you more than my words can.

The food in a Maya village is very good. It is all fresh and natural. Most families have their own chickens and turkeys and some raise pigs too. The land in this part of Yucatán doesn't provide enough grass to feed cattle, so a good hamburger is a rare thing in a village. They make wonderful soups and stews like shredded chicken with carrots, potatoes, and squash in a broth. There is always a lot of fresh fruits in season. All of it is very tasty and very healthy. One of my favorite foods is *polcanes*. *Polcan* is Maya for the head of a snake! They are not really snake heads, but are like a corn meal hush puppy filled with white beans and onions. We drank tamarind and grapefruit juices and two different milky drinks, one made from rice and the other from oats.

Sleeping in a Maya village is a new experience. The people are poor and cannot afford to build houses or huts with many rooms that only have one purpose like a living room or a bedroom. So they build huts for multiple purposes. One hut will serve as a living room, a workshop, and a bedroom. You can't have beds filling up the living room, so they don't use them. They sleep in hammocks that can be flipped up over a beam during the day when they need the room for another purpose. A prosperous Maya may have several huts: one for sleeping and a living room, another for cooking and eating, one for hammock weaving, and another for storing corn and beans harvested from the fields.

The Yucatec Maya of today are a very warm, friendly, and happy people, even the poorest of the poor out in the jungle.

The next day we went to the ruins of the ancient city of Chichen Itza. It has just been named one of the new seven wonders of the world. Your Maestra (teacher) has been to Chichen Itza and can tell you about it. Two thousand years ago, Chichen Itza was a very powerful and important religious and government center for the Yucatec Maya. Several hundred thousand people lived and worshiped there. Many of the magnificent temples and pyramids have been restored for us to see. An amazing thing about all of the ancient cities is that they were built by hand without machines, electric or gas-powered tools, or even beasts of burden like horses or oxen to carry things. As I said before, the ancient Maya were great astronomers. The buildings are perfectly aligned with various stars, and by tracking the sun, they can

Temple Kukulcan at Chichen Itza, one of the new seven wonders of the world

The Maya Observatory at Chichen Itza

be used as a perfect calendar. I say perfect calendar because our calendar isn't perfect since we need to add an extra day every four years (Leap Year) to make it accurate. The Maya building/calendar doesn't need a leap year. Two thousand years ago, they were smarter than we are today with all our computers, telescopes, etc.

After our visit to Chichen Itza, we went to a *cenote* named Ik Kil. It was seventy-five feet under the ground. Everyone went swimming in it except me. Being made of cardboard, I need to be careful around water.

Ik Kil Cenote

Oxkintok

Oxkintok ("owesh-keen-toke") is not famous like Chichen Itza, but what I liked most about visiting there was that there were no other people there. It was like we discovered it ourselves and had it all to ourselves. That is a neat feeling. It was an important link on the ancient Maya trade route. It is also more scenic. While Chichen Itza sits on a huge piece of flat land, Oxkintok sits in a valley surrounded by tree-covered hills.

Uxmal

All of the other ruins we have seen have had mixed architecture of Maya and Aztec. Uxmal ("ooosh-mal") is the only ancient site of pure Maya architecture. The main temple, the Temple of the magician, has rounded instead of sharp corners, very unusual. While Chichen Itza has buildings like the Palace of the Warriors or a building to cut out the hearts of the enemy, Uxmal has building like the Dove Cote and a House of Turtles. It also has a rather large quadrangle with a dormitory or bedrooms built all the way around. Some of the buildings are very pretty. Like the other sites, Uxmal also has a ball court, but it is smaller than some of the others.

I have mentioned ball courts a few times. These courts were not used for tennis or baseball or football or even for soccer which is very popular here. The Maya had their own ball game. The sides of the ball courts were lined with very tall walls with a big stone circle sticking out high up in the middle of the wall. The court at Chichen Itza is 750 feet long and 260 feet wide, much bigger than a football field. The walls are thirty-three feet high and the circle is about twenty feet high. The objective is to knock a ball

The ball court at Chichen Itza

through the circle, like basketball, only the circle is vertical instead of horizontal. It sounds easy enough, but there are a couple of things that make it difficult. One is that you couldn't use your hands or feet, only your knees, legs, hips, and elbows. The other thing was that the ball was made of a heavy rubber. You certainly didn't want to use your head like we do in soccer to be hitting a heavy ball! I imagine that using your knees and elbows would hurt a lot, too. They did wear pads on their hips and probably jerked their padded hips to hit the ball more than anything else.

They carved the results of the games on the walls using glyphs. You can still see those glyphs today. I was trying to interpret one of the glyphs, I think it read; Chichen Itza Eagles 2, the Oxkintok Giants 0. There is a debate about what happened to the winners and losers of the games. What seems to be certain is that somebody was going to be sacrificed to the gods. My own theory is that the winners were probably taller than the losers; it was easier for them because they were taller. That means that the losers were the short guys. I think that they wanted to honor their gods by giving the very best, the taller winners, and that is why today, most Maya are very short. I met a lot of adult Maya that are less than five feet tall.

The Temple of the Inscriptions

The Pakal Tomb

Do you remember that during the trip to Yucatán we went through a place called Chiapas where the Zapatistas had a rebellion and Ozzie had jumped at the solders' faces? I said that we would return with some college students. Well today, January 15th, we do just that. We had a big bus all to ourselves and drove most of the day to the town of Palenque. Palenque is the last town before we would go back up into the mountains. We spent two nights at a hotel there. The day after we arrived, we went to the ruins of the ancient Maya city of Palenque. The Palenque ruins are older than the other sites that we have visited by a few hundred years. It is quite stunning in appearance, with many of the buildings located in lush green, not hills like Oxkintok, but mountain sides. The Temple of the Inscriptions has, way deep inside, a tomb of their greatest king that is very big and covered with glyphs For almost two thousand years, no one could read or interpret the glyphs. About twenty years ago, someone finally broke the code of the glyphs, and we learned a lot about the history of Palenque from them. It is too much information to share here. I bought a book that tells a lot more about the Maya.

You may wonder why we rode a bus all day just to see more

ancient city ruins and visit more Maya people. Well, the reason is that we have only visited things in the state of Yucatán, the Yucatec Maya, but there are twenty-five different kinds of Maya and Maya languages. While the Yucatán has only one kind of Maya, the state of Chiapas has seven different kinds of Maya and Maya languages. Let me see if I can remember all of them . . . the

Tzotzil and Tzeltal live in the northern part of Chiapas, the Lacandon (who speak Yucatec Maya) live in the jungle the Chol, Zoque and Tojolabal live in the west and southern parts, and the Mam live on the southern coast.

Tonina

We will see mostly Tzeltal around Palenque, maybe a Lacandon, and then visit two Tzotzil villages in the mountains.

The last ancient ruin that we visited was Tonina. Did we see all of the ancient cities? Not quite. It is estimated that there are over twelve thousand ancient sites in Mexico, so we still have 11,994 to see! Tonina is south of Palenque, deeper into the mountains and jungle, and closer to the country of Guatemala. While it is not as well known as the other sites that we visited, it is equally impressive. It has towering temples in one large structure, had a history of being very warlike, and conquered other Maya cities. Their greatest king even called himself "He of Many Captives."

After visiting Tonina we continued driving south and west into the mountains. Remember when Nojoch K'ai, Ozzie, and I came over the mountains? It took us five hours in the car. It took the bus a whole lot longer, and it didn't go as far as we did in the car. Remembering that drive, I am reminded of Ozzie and wonder how he is doing with Nojoch K'ai being gone for a week. I bet that he is really glad to see Lucia every day!

We arrived safely in the city of San Cristobal. Actually

its real name is San Cristobal de las Casas, which means "St. Christopher of the Houses." It is a small, but very busy city in the mountains.

An interesting thing about the Maya of Chiapas is that each village has its own special clothes that most of the people wear. If you memorize all the different costumes of the villages, you can tell where someone is from just by the way that they dress. Another difference with the Maya of Chiapas is that they try to keep the old traditions while the Maya of Yucatán use modern things in their lives. In the streets of San Cristobal, you can see many different costumes of the many people that come in from the villages to shop or go to government offices for help. These Maya in San Cristobal are the Tzotzil Maya, and they work very hard at preserving their traditions of several hundred years.

The old chapel in San Juan Chamula

Tzotzil Maya of San Juan Chamula

The following day, we went out into the mountain villages of San Juan Chamula and Zinacantan. San Juan Chamula is a village that serves as the religious and government center for many smaller villages in the mountains. In the USA, we are free to have whatever religious beliefs we want to have. In San Juan Chamula, you either believe the ancient Maya way or they throw you out! The chapel that used to be a Catholic church is now a building where the *H'men* (healers) sit on the straw-covered floor with candles and bottles of a special alcohol and heal their village clients. They recite chants and rub eggs on the sick people and get the Maya spirits to heal them. They also use herbs and plants for healing. If you take a photograph in here, they will throw you in jail, so I didn't take any photos!

There is a common belief about the Maya that they believe that if you take their photograph, it takes part of their spirit away. That may or may not be true, but this is what Nojoch K'ai says about it. How would you like it if every time you went out of your house someone took your picture because they thought that you were unusual or different or odd or funny-looking like a freak show at a carnival? It isn't respectful to treat people like that, and maybe all they want is to be treated with respect. I know that I don't want to be treated that way.

Zinacantan was a lot like San Juan Chamula except it was more open to foreigners and photographs. The people were more friendly and shared their lives more with us, more like the villagers of Tinum did back in Yucatán.

Juana Perez weaving cloth

Some of her work in Zinacantan

The custom of having distinct clothing for each village led to an interesting activity. The country of Guatemala is next door to the mountains and jungles of Chiapas and the same kinds of Maya live there. Several years ago the government of Guatemala was very bad and often would attack people from different villages, and they could identify them because of their clothing. So many of the Maya who feared for their lives

Flat Stanley joined the Zapatista Rebellion (not really—just a Flat Stanley joke).

very carefully took their clothes apart and rewove the threads into cloth bags, purses, table-cloths, and other things and sold them to tourists to make money for food and different clothing that the government would not recognize. Pretty clever, huh?

Today is January 25th and I am leaving Nojoch K'ai and Ozzie in Yucatán and flying back to North Carolina with the students. Then I will be mailed to my friend Zyon in Pennsylvania. This journey has taken about ten weeks and has covered more than eight thousand miles. I saw a lot of the United States and Mexico. I got to know people whose families have been in the Yucatán for more than five thousand years. I visited ancient Maya cities with their magnificent buildings and I got to know some Yucatec and Tzotzil Maya. I learned why there is no other place on earth like the peninsula of Yucatán. Through the Maya I came to know, to understand, and to feel the heart and soul of this special place.

My friend Zyon, thank you so much for sending me on this journey. It was incredible! I hope that you will enjoy sharing my adventures with the other children in your class.

Adios, Nojoch K'ai and Ozzie.

Flat Stanley

Written by Flat Stanley for his friend Zyon

About the Publisher

With great pleasure, The Write Place assisted Alan Van Bodegraven in accomplishing his goal: making a book from the wonderful essays he had written over the years so that readers could experience the Yucatán with him and see it through his eyes. Through publishing *Adventures in Contemporary Yucatán,* he shares his experiences and vision with the wider world; he leaves a legacy for his family to treasure.

The Write Place staff members enjoy assisting writers realize their publication dreams, and we provide as little or as much help as writers desire. Our service range includes ghost-writing, editing, proofreading, layout, cover design, printing, and some publicity services.

For more information, email us at query@thewriteplace.biz or call 641-628-8398 for a 15-minute, no obligation consultation.

Printed in the United States
145714LV00002B/28/P

9 780980 008432